*The Awakening Church*

# The Awakening Church

25 Years of Liturgical Renewal

*Edited by*
*Lawrence J. Madden, S.J.*

*A Liturgical Press Book*

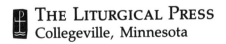
THE LITURGICAL PRESS
Collegeville, Minnesota

Cover design by Greg Becker.

| 1 | 2 | 3 | 4 | 5 | 6 | 7 | 8 | 9 |
|---|---|---|---|---|---|---|---|---|

**Library of Congress Cataloging-in-Publication Data**

The Awakening church / edited by Lawrence J. Madden.
     p.    cm.
   Papers presented at a colloquium held Dec. 3–5, 1988 at Georgetown University.
   Includes bibliographical references.
   ISBN 0-8146-2031-0
   1. Catholic Church—United States—Liturgy—History—20th century-
-Congresses.  I. Madden, Lawrence J.
   BX1970.A1A93  1992
   264'.02'00973'09045—dc20                        91-42504
                                                         CIP

*To those in the American Church*
*who seek to promote the worship of God*
*both in spirit and in truth*

# Contents

# Acknowledgments

On behalf of the liturgists who undertook this study I want to express our deep gratitude to James Lopresti. He alone of our group had enough knowledge, though he insisted it was nonprofessional, of the social sciences to enable us to dream of attempting such a project. We are most grateful to him for his wisdom and optimism. He is the person most responsible for the design of the study that produced the papers in this volume.

Next must be thanked the pastors, staffs, and parishioners of the fifteen parishes whose liturgies we studied. They welcomed us into their lives and shared with openness and honesty their thoughts, difficulties, and prayers. They became symbols of hope for us.

I would like to thank Rev. Charles L. Currie, S.J., the director of Georgetown University's bicentennial celebration, who showed such strong, early interest in the project, and to Mr. A. G. McCarthy of the Loyola Foundation, whose financial support made the colloquium possible.

I wish to acknowledge with deep gratitude the contributions of Rev. Andrew Ciferni, O. Prem., Sr. Jan Schlichting, O.P., and Sr. Jennifer Glen, C.C.V.I., who served on the planning committee for the colloquium; the Norbertine Community of Daylesford Abbey, who hosted the committee's first meeting; Ms. Lorraine Strope and Mr. Robert Williams, who provided administrative support; Sauder Church Furniture, Inc., J. S. Paluch Company, GIA Publications, and Will and Baumer, Inc., for their generous support of the colloquium.

Special thanks are due to the scholars whose papers form the substance of this volume and to all our wise and devoted guests who came to the colloquium, where these papers were first presented and discussed.

I wish to thank the staff members of the sponsoring liturgical centers for their stimulating colleagueship, their firm commitment to the project, and their good counsel. They and those they enlisted to aid them carried the major burden of the collection and transcription of data that formed the base of the study. Among this group I must single out Mr. Paul Covino of The Georgetown Center for Liturgy, Spirituality, and the Arts for special thanks. Without his organizing talent and gracious attentiveness the colloquium would not have been such a success.

Finally, I wish to thank Ms. Barbara Conley Waldmiller, my assistant, for her cheerful and competent assistance in preparing the manuscript.

Lawrence J. Madden, S.J.

# Introduction

On the weekend of December third through fifth, 1988, a colloquium was held at Georgetown University to celebrate the twenty-fifth anniversary of The Constitution on the Sacred Liturgy of Vatican Council II. In attendance were Bishops Joseph Delaney and John Snyder, respectively chair and member of the Bishops' Committee on the Liturgy, along with some two hundred invited participants. These were directors of diocesan offices of worship or liturgical commissions, members of seminary and university faculties, pastors and parishioners from fifteen parishes who participated in the study that led to the colloquium, and other guests with special expertise or experience in the field of pastoral liturgy.

The participants came to hear and respond to nine scholars from various disciplines, all having a particular bearing on the study of the liturgy. The scholars' task was to attempt to judge the degree of success or lack thereof of the liturgical reforms of the council in American parishes in the twenty-five years since the promulgation of The Constitution on the Sacred Liturgy. As a focus and stimulus for the scholars' reflection a study had been conducted by four American liturgical centers: The Notre Dame Center for Pastoral Liturgy, the Georgetown Center for Liturgy, Spirituality, and the Arts, The Loyola Pastoral Institute, and the Corpus Christi Center. Fifteen parishes from various areas of the United States were selected for the study. These parishes were selected because they had demonstrated a sustained interest in implementing the reform of the liturgy and because they represented a cross section of the English-speaking American Church. Because of staff limitations, the centers were not able to include Hispanic parishes in the study.

It is important to understand the kind of data the nine scholars had at their disposal. The study was what is refered to as an "insight stimulation'' study. Much data was assembled on the parishes' liturgical programs and celebrations. Some of it could be subjected to statistical analysis, but most of it could not. The study was not intended to produce hard statistical data; it was intended to be a stimulus to the scholars, providing them with a broad range of data, including photographs of the Churches, testimonies from planners and participants, and descriptions from visiting participant-observers. The wealth of insight one finds in the papers of the colloquium presented in this volume and the genuine excitement and satisfaction at the colloquium itself amply demonstrate that the project achieved substantial success.

Being one of the first studies of this nature attempted in Catholic parishes, along with its strengths it also showed some weaknesses. But some of the scholars, while pointing out the nature of those weaknesses, were able to make constructive suggestions for further study.

The first seven papers collected in this volume formed the substance of the colloquium. (Another presentation, that of William McCready, is not included here.) After each two presentations the colloquium participants, seated at round tables, had an opportunity to discuss among themselves the material presented.

On the final morning of the colloquium three presentations were given: two short presentations followed by one major address. The first short presentation was delivered by Peter Henriot, S.J., of the Center of Concern. Because of the importance of the linkage of faith with justice, Father Henriot was invited to the colloquium and was asked to speak to this issue after hearing all the major presentations.

The second short presentation was by Juan Sosa of the Institute for Hispanic Liturgy. Although the centers that conducted the study were not able to survey solely Hispanic-speaking parishes, still, because of the size and importance of the Spanish-speaking Church in America, Father Sosa was also invited to attend the colloquium and to address the participants after the major addresses.

The final major address was delivered by Dr. Kathleen Hughes. Dr. Hughes was invited to perform a special service for the participants in the colloquium. She was invited to listen to all the major addresses, to participate in the discussions and then at the conclusion of the event to address the assembly on the subject of the future of liturgical reform in America. It was a task she performed with admirable aplomb.

The papers in this volume begin with that of Ronald Grimes, an expert in ritual studies, who divided his presentation into two parts. One does not have to be a seasoned social scientist to profit from the incisive observations Dr. Grimes makes in the first part of his paper, where he critiques the study itself. While his ideas will certainly help scholars refine the process of studying religious ritual in parish life, his remarks will also be helpful for all those who are engaged in the ministry of liturgical worship and who attempt periodically to assess the effectiveness of their work.

In the second part of his paper he goes beyond the study document itself and attempts to assess the rites that were studied. The author speaks from extensive experience in ritual participation and from years of serious study. His observations of Catholic worship, such as "So much is aimed at the eye and ear and so little at belly and foot," deserve a serious hearing by liturgists.

Roger Haight, in his paper, explores how the liturgy mediates grace. Starting with principles derived from the theology of grace, he finds some of them exemplified or concretized in the data of the study. He then uses these principles to critically reflect on the significance of that data. Liturgy, according to Haight, is an ordinary event in human life whose immediate purpose is "to bring grace to conscious expression."

Gerard Sloyan comments on the data in the study in the light of the Christologies inherent in it. He does not refrain from critiquing the Christology imbedded in our current official liturgical texts and argues for a more balanced Christological statement of belief closer in the style of expression to that of the Council of Chalcedon. Of particular interest should be the fact that in the liturgies studied he finds no evidence of the Christologies being formed at the present time by the sufferings of the dispossessed or by the sense of alienation experienced by Western Christian women.

Monika Hellwig addresses the subject from the point of view of ecclesiology. She selects for comment six particular directions of change in the post–Vatican II Church. She relates these shifts in direction to the testimonies of people in the parishes studied. Then she considers the chief emphases in the ecclesiology of Vatican II that seem to validate these shifts as authentic developments. Finally, she suggests some pastoral and liturgical implications for the future. While being somewhat critical of certain developments in the parishes, Hellwig concludes that the study shows "what a splendid beginning has been made in some parishes, which can then serve as models for others."

It is as a specialist in the theory of symbol that Don Saliers addresses the material in the study. He proposes that we have to reas-

sess how we have conceived and fostered liturgical participation. He
notes that one looks in vain in the data for references to the sense of
transcendent mystery in the expression of primary symbol, and he feels
that too much focus has been placed on the "expressive" dimensions
of participation rather than on the inner relations between the formative and expressive power of primary symbol. He suggests that "perhaps the greatest task ahead of us in light of the data from this survey
is to restore a sense of history and *mysterion* to the symbols embedded
in the ritual action of the liturgy."

Aidan Kavanagh's paper places the liturgical state reported by the
study within the historical stream of Christian liturgical practice. From
this point of view he discovers several characteristics of present practice that give cause for concern. These include a notion of "community" that needs to be critically examined; a "gathering rite" phenomenon, which instead of being a rite of prayer and processional entry has become a rite of hospitality inviting people into "community";
little sense of the transcendence of God in the liturgies reported; and
"an incredible lightness of doctrine," especially in respect to the holiness of God and the sinfulness of human beings.

John Baldovin reviews the data of the survey from the point of view
of pastoral liturgical theology. Keeping an eye on the social and psycho-
logical conditions that prevail in today's world, Baldovin reflects on
the various sacramental images that the survey surfaces. He sounds
some serious warnings about the conception people have of the role
of the liturgy in their lives. He then discusses three fundamental issues in pastoral practice that the survey raises: the way the Eucharistic Prayer is proclaimed, the proclamation of the word, and, finally,
what the author calls "the importance of liturgy," meaning the degree of conviction in evidence that the ritual symbols of Christian faith
are crucial for truly human life in the world.

In his short paper Peter Henriot's major thesis is that there is an
integral link between liturgy and life, between the celebration of liturgy
and the doing of justice. This link, he explains, is empirically verified
in the history of the American liturgical movement. He highlights a
number of key issues raised by the major speakers of the colloquium,
wonders at the absence of certain justice issues in the evidence, and,
finally, makes some recommendations for further study of the effectiveness of the liturgy.

Juan Sosa, in his short presentation, outlines the key issues in liturgical reform as seen by one who, as director of the Instituto de Litur-

gia Hispana for ten years, has traveled extensively throughout the United States to help Hispanic communities implement the reforms of Vatican II. He links liturgical issues in multilanguage parishes to social-cultural issues as he explains the two principal areas of the Instituto's concerns: integration of the Hispanic communities into American society and enculturation of the liturgy.

Kathleen Hughes, in the colloquium's final address, looks for signs of hope as she examines the survey's data in dialogue with the remarks of the other speakers. Maintaining that the future agenda must be built on the bedrock of our present strength, Hughes outlines the reasons she discovers for great hope. Finally, she suggests an agenda for the future work in liturgical renewal.

### Description of the Study

The following is a description of how the reports on each parish were generated and prepared by the centers sponsoring the study.

There were three major sections in each report.

1. The first section, "Parish Background," contained a summary of facts collected in a survey questionnaire completed by the pastor or associate pastor of the parish.

2. The second section, "Parish Liturgy Program Description and Evaluation," was a distillation of data the centers collected in four areas:

   *a.* The liturgical ministries of the parish

   *b.* The liturgy planning process in the parish

   *c.* The musical, artistic, and environmental aspects of the parish liturgical program

   *d.* An evaluation of the parish liturgical program done by the parish staff.

3. The third section, "Description and Evaluation of a Particular Sunday Liturgy," was in three parts:

   *a.* This part contains two reports on the liturgy celebrated in each parish.

The first report is offered by the parish director of liturgy. It describes *the usual structure* of a Sunday Eucharist at the parish.

The second report is a distillation of notes taken by a participant-observer of the liturgy. The frame for those notes is a replication of the participant-observer schedule used by the Notre Dame Study of Catholic Parish Life.

The liturgies contained in this report occurred on particular Sundays in autumn of 1987. These specific liturgies were chosen because they each represented one of the best efforts of the parishes participating in the study.

b. This part contained a transcribed interview with two parishioners who met with the participant-observer immediately after the liturgy observed. The parishioners were invited to recall their "inner experiences" of the liturgy just celebrated. To gain that perspective, the researcher invited them to re-live, section by section, the liturgy in which they had just participated. After a quieting exercise, the researcher cued the respondent with phrases to recall the moments of the Eucharist just celebrated. The respondent was asked to report all that he or she could remember about that moment.

An attempt was made to include one "more active" parishioner and one "less active" parishioner in these interviews. "More active" meant someone who not only worshiped regularly at this parish but also frequently took on roles in the liturgy. "Less active" meant someone who regularly worshiped in this parish but did not serve in any ministerial role in the liturgy.

c. The third part was a transcribed interview held with the presider at that liturgy, the parish liturgy director, and the director of music at that liturgy. This interview was scheduled about a week after the liturgy observed. In advance of this interview the researcher had the respondents fill out a questionnaire, which was studied and used by the researcher to probe for further clarification and elaboration.

## Parishes That Participated in the Study

*Saint Mary of the Isle,* Diocese of Rockville Center, New York.

Saint Mary of the Isle is one of two territorial parishes located in the small city of Long Beach. It is served by diocesan clergy. Total attendance at Masses on an average Sunday is between 1,000 and 1,500.

This community is composed primarily of persons of Hispanic origin and secondarily of those of European origin. Between 25% and 50% of the parishioners are foreign born. Liturgies are celebrated in both English and Spanish.

*Saint Brigid,* Diocese of Rockville Center, New York.

Saint Brigid is a territorial parish located in a high-density suburban area and staffed by diocesan clergy. Total attendance at Masses on an average Sunday is over 2,500.

The majority of the parishioners are of European descent. Of the remainder a substantial minority are Hispanic. Although less than 25% of the parishioners are foreign born, Masses are celebrated in Spanish, Korean, Italian, and English.

*The Franciscan Renewal Center,* Diocese of Phoenix, Arizona.

The Franciscan Renewal Center is a nonterritorial parish located in an urban resort area and staffed by religious clergy. Total attendance on an average Sunday is between 1,500 and 2,500.

The Center's community is predominantly of European descent with the majority of the rest being Hispanic. Less than 25% of the congregation is foreign born.

*Saint Augustine,* Archdiocese of Washington, District of Columbia.

Saint Augustine is a territorial parish that draws parishioners from a wide area. It is located in an inner-city neighborhood. Total attendance on an average Sunday is between 1,000 and 1,500.

Saint Augustine's parishioners are predominantly African-American; fewer than 25% are foreign born. English is the only language used in the liturgy.

*Saint Amant,* Diocese of Baton Rouge, Louisiana.

Saint Amant is a territorial parish located in a rural area and staffed by diocesan clergy. Total attendance on an average Sunday is between 1,000 and 1,500.

Almost all of the parishioners are of French-Acadian descent. Few are foreign born. English is the only language used in the liturgy.

*Holy Redeemer,* Diocese of Grand Rapids, Michigan.

Holy Redeemer is a territorial parish located in a high-density suburban area and staffed by diocesan clergy. Total attendance on Sunday is about 2,500.

The community is almost entirely of European origin, and fewer than 25% are foreign born. English is the only language used in the liturgy.

*Holy Trinity,* Archdiocese of Washington, District of Columbia.

Holy Trinity is a territorial parish that draws parishioners from a wide area. It is located in a residential urban area and is staffed by religious clergy. The average attendance on Sundays is between 3,000 and 3,500.

Most of Holy Trinity's parishioners are of European origin. Fewer than 25% are foreign born. English is the only language used in the liturgy.

*Saint Gregory the Great,* Diocese of Brooklyn, New York.

Saint Gregory the Great is a territorial parish located in the inner city of Brooklyn and is staffed by diocesan clergy. Total attendance on an average Sunday ranges between 500 and 1,000.

The majority of the parishioners are West Indian and the remainder are Hispanic. Between 50% and 75% are foreign born. English is the only language used in the liturgy.

*Cathedral of the Sacred Heart,* Diocese of Richmond, Virginia.

The Cathedral of the Sacred Heart is located in Richmond's inner-city area. It is a territorial parish that draws members from the entire city. The staff includes one diocesan priest and four laypeople. Total attendance on an average Sunday is between 1,000 and 1,500.

Most parishioners are of European origin with the remainder being African-American. Fewer than 25% are foreign born. English is the only language used in the liturgy.

*Church of the Incarnation,* Diocese of Richmond, Virginia.

The Church of the Incarnation is the only territorial parish in Albemarle County, Virginia. It embraces high- and low-density suburban areas as well as a large rural area. It is staffed by diocesan clergy. Average attendance on Sunday is between 1,000 and 1,500.

Most members of this community are of European origin; there are a few of Asian origin. Fewer than 25% are foreign born. English is the only language used in the liturgy.

*Christ The King,* Diocese of Reno–Las Vegas, Nevada.

Christ the King is a territorial parish located in a low-density suburban area of Las Vegas and staffed by diocesan clergy. Average Sunday attendance is about 2,500.

Most parishioners are of European origin; there is a significant percentage of Hispanic parishioners. Fewer than 25% are foreign born.

*Saint Augustine,* Diocese of Phoenix, Arizona.

Saint Augustine is a territorial parish located in a high-density suburban area and staffed by diocesan clergy. Total attendance on an average Sunday is between 1,000 and 1,500.

Most parishioners are of European descent; a significant number are Hispanic. Less than 25% are foreign born. Both English and Spanish are used in the liturgy.

*Saint Barbara,* Archdiocese of Chicago, Illinois.

Saint Barbara is a territorial parish in a high-density suburban area and is staffed by diocesan clergy. Total attendance on an average Sunday is over 2,500.

Parishioners are predominantly of European origin and fewer than 25% are foreign born. English is the only language used in the liturgy.

*Saint Timothy,* Diocese of Phoenix, Arizona.

Saint Timothy is a territorial parish located in a high-density urban area that draws many people from the surrounding area. It is staffed by two diocesan clergy and one religious priest. The average Sunday attendance is about 5,000.

About 90% of the parishioners are of European descent; the remainder are Hispanic, Asian, and African-American. English is the only language used in the liturgy.

*Bellarmine Chapel,* Archdiocese of Cincinnati, Ohio.

Bellarmine Chapel is a nonterritorial community located on a college campus in an urban area. It is staffed by religious clergy. Total attendance on an average Sunday is between 1,000 and 1,500.

Members are mostly of European origin; a small number are African-American. Fewer than 25% are foreign born. English is the only language used in the liturgy.

## The Centers for Liturgy

*The Notre Dame Center for Pastoral Liturgy,* established by the American bishops in 1970 as a national liturgical center, is committed to fostering dialogue between liturgical scholarship and pastoral practice, between Christian tradition and the challenges of the present. Through its educational programs, publications, and research, the Center reaches out to those who serve as leaders in the worship life of the American Church. The national week-long conference at Notre Dame focuses on a liturgical theme of current import. Workshops are held throughout the year, both on the university campus and at designated locations across the country. In addition, the Center's resources also include *Assembly*, a short periodical exploring the tradition, meaning, and practice of a single topic, a *Pastoral Liturgy Bibliography*, and the proceedings of its conferences. The staff includes Sr. Eleanor Bernstein, C.S.J., Dr. John Brooks-Leonard, and Dr. Nathan D. Mitchell. *Box 81, Notre Dame, IN 46556, 219-239-5435*

*The Georgetown Center for Liturgy, Spirituality, and the Arts*, founded jointly in 1981 by Georgetown University and Holy Trinity Parish, is a teaching, research, and pastoral reflection institute working with parishes to enhance the quality of their worship. The Center conducts regular regional workshops in Washington and Boston, national conferences, including a conference on environment for worship every eighteen months, programs for parishes and dioceses, special programs for the clergy, and offers a certificate program in liturgical studies at Georgetown University. The faculty includes Rev. Lawrence Madden, S.J., Mr. Paul Covino, and Rev. Paul Cioffi, S.J. *3513 N Street, NW, Washington, DC 20007, 202-687-4420*

*The Loyola Pastoral Institute* provides a forum for pastoral reflection on the liturgy for the Roman Catholic community in the Greater New York area. The programs of the Institute are offered by the faculty of the Seminary of the Immaculate Conception, professional liturgists residing in the Greater New York area, and guest liturgists. The offerings of the Institute include opportunities for advanced research in conjunction with the Seminary's Doctor of Ministry and Masters programs, on-site study weeks, and workshops throughout the New York area. The Institute's programs address a wide audience within the Roman Catholic community and provide service to those involved in the common prayer of the Christian community. Director of the Institute is Sr. Mary Alice Piil, C.S.J., a member of the faculty of the Seminary of the Immaculate Conception. *440 West Neck Road, Huntington, NY 11743, 516-673-2238*

*The Corpus Christi Center for Liturgy*, founded by Rev. John Gallen, S.J., was a liturgical resource to parishes in the southwestern United States. Recently the programs and resources of the Center have been moved to Resource Publications. *160 E. Virginia Street #290, San Jose, CA 95112, 408-286-8505*

# Liturgical Renewal and Ritual Criticism

## Ronald L. Grimes

Unguarded utterances by ritual participants ought to be a *sine qua non* of all ritological interpretation and theological reflection. Three such candid, unlabored utterances from *Liturgical Renewal, 1963–1988: A Study of English Speaking Parishes in the United States* (hereafter referred to as *LR*) mark the boundaries of my reflections. The first suggests how much rides on a liturgy: "We kind of have to do this," says one person, "because if we don't, we're not."

The second implies that, upon this twenty-fifth anniversary of The Constitution on the Sacred Liturgy, the honeymoon is over and the limitations of this great liturgical reform are now tangible. As a participant in the study puts it, "Everyone never does everything together." (I am so taken by this sentiment that I am sure I'll be tempted to chant it during Christmas family get-togethers.)

A third quotation indicates why it is so difficult to study and assess a rite. This person remarks, "[The liturgy] is highly familiar and easily ignored." The most important aspects of liturgies are often invisible, not just to outsiders but also to insiders who take them for granted.

So, however true it is that if we don't do it, we're not, it is also true that everyone never does everything together, and even if they did, their actions would soon become so familiar that they could easily be ignored. This is why the liturgy must be subject to ongoing criticism. And this is why, as your "professional ignorant observer" (as my wife tags my job at this conference), my job is to call attention to the obvious, which is so easily ignored.

The editors of *Worship*, one of the most respected North American scholarly journals on liturgy, recently wrote:

11

As worshiping communities continue to internalize the meaning of the extensive liturgical reforms that have taken place in the last twenty-five years, to evaluate critically the effectiveness of those reforms and to search for new rituals that enable worshipers to praise and serve God amidst the rapidly changing cultural patterns in the world, we are convinced that we should continue to concentrate on a theoretic approach to liturgical issues. This does not mean that we shall not be concerned with practical matters. As experience has shown, the doctrinal study of liturgy is often best situated at the level of concrete ritual structures and explicit pastoral problems. Liturgical materials of all kinds are being issued at the present time, many of which would be better left unpublished. There is a great need to provide liturgists with sound criteria for evaluating what appears on the market from both popular and official sources (*Worship* 61 (1) [1987] 80).

In keeping with this aim I will spend most of my time reflecting critically and theoretically upon *LR*, but first there are some obvious strengths in this study that deserve to be summarized: (1) That this was done at all, that a concerted effort was made to assess one of the hardest cultural forms to evaluate, liturgy, is remarkable. (2) The scale of the study is considerable; it clearly reflects much commitment, devotion, and energy. (3) The research involved many kinds of people: lay, clergy, less-active and more-active parishioners, scholars, and church staff. (4) It records some actual words of participants and attempts to document actually enacted rites. (5) It attempts to formulate and apply an instrument for the study of liturgy. (6) And it submits itself to critical scrutiny and ongoing revision.

Critical self-studies by religious bodies are rare; those aimed specifically at liturgical rites, even rarer. Any group that attempts systematic ritual criticism deserves commendation. One must also be impressed that the Church would invite non–Roman Catholics to contribute substantially to the evaluation process, because liturgy is that aspect of religion that is usually the most heavily guarded, thus making discussions of it the most in-house.

Faced with a ritual account, a student of ritual ought to reflect on the document that presents it before proceeding to the ritual as such. Insisting on this is no different from insisting that the New Testament does not present us with Jesus as such but with Matthew's Jesus, Mark's Jesus—in short, with a community's image of a person, not with "the man himself." As a vigorous advocate of field study, I am now in the ironic position of having to suffer the way historians of religion suffer: I am asked not only to infer enactments from a text but also to evaluate enactments on the basis of someone else's text.

## The Text of the Study

Although I have attended Masses and even studied them in the context of Hispanic Catholicism in New Mexico, I simply do not have regular access to post-Vatican II liturgies. So in the beginning I decided to make it a matter of discipline to bracket out everything but the written materials at hand and to ask, What image of liturgy emerges from these pages? The result was that I probably took people's words more seriously than they took them. What I arrived at is not liturgy as such but the ways laypeople, priests, and Catholic scholars imagine and narrate liturgy. Unless imagining and narrating are regarded as unimportant constituents of a people's sense of ritual, this procedure tells us something important about the liturgies themselves. It tells us, to use Kantian language, in terms of what categories of imagination rites are constructed.

Because of the way the document before us was conceived and produced, one has to view enacted and observed liturgies through multiple layers. Each of the following layers enhances and distorts our vision of these liturgies:

> *The Instrument*—the questions, checklists, and other devices used on-site to evoke memories, reflections, and judgments about recollected rites;
>
> *The Document*—the reports as organized, summarized, prefaced, and edited by staff, editors, and ghost writers at the four sponsoring liturgy centers;
>
> *Participants' memories and perceptions*—the rites as selectively perceived and partially remembered by those who filled out the forms and wrote the reports as directed by the instrument;
>
> *The texts*—the liturgical writings and directives that formed the liturgical enactments;
>
> *The rites*—the liturgical enactments themselves, which, like all performative genres, are performed in a particular time and place and then, at least socially and humanly considered, are no more (except as "residue" in texts, memories, and documents).

In addition to the multiplicity of mediating devices, there are other difficulties with the study, which I can only summarize here:[1]

Section 1, parish background, is so cursory with its demographics that it is difficult to use them for grounding one's assessment. "The facts" are so impressionistic that one is unsure how far to trust them. The photographs help a little, but they are mostly of buildings, not of parish life or liturgical activity.

Sections 2 and 3, liturgical ministries and planning, consist of lists that identify operative roles and questions about training and consultation but little about the felt or lived qualities of either.

Section 4, music, art, and environment, by virtue of being a separate section from those on the liturgy itself, seems to imply their ancillary nature. And even if this is not the case, the sections do not inquire about either the effects or qualities of art. What we need is a description of places, objects, and events that focuses on their qualities and textures. Instead we have one-word or one-sentence answers to questions. Unfortunately, we are given no ethnographic-style descriptions, so we learn little about the liturgical environment inside the church or the social and ecological environment outside it.

Section 5, the liturgy program, although it aims at evaluation, asks for lists. People's responses are not pursued; implications do not emerge; secondary matters are not separated from primary ones.

Section 6, the liturgy directors' reports, are so formed by the research instrument and thus so typified that the liturgies appear much more uniform than I suspect they really are. What we need instead is an attempt to depict what we might call "the indigenous style" of each parish's worship. Assuming that considerable consistency and uniformity is desirable and in fact operative in liturgies, we still need to know what is distinctive about the tone, tenor, and ambience of each parish's celebrations. Conveying such qualities is a difficult task, but it is essential if we want to take account of the localization and indigenization of liturgy and not just its universalization.

Section 7, the participant-observers' reports, lack both the refreshing naiveté of outsiders and the authoritative expertise of specialists. The rhetoric is so uniform that one can only suspect that editorial reworking stands between us and the parishioners' perceptions. Not only is there no concentration on the living quality of a specific celebration, most of the participant-observers are missing from their own reports, so we have no idea how to make allowances for their biases. The action is described generically. There are no embodied actors, only roles. No one sneezes in these liturgies. The air has no temperature or smell. The walls have no color, the garments no texture.

Section 8, the recall interviews, because they allow us to see how a researcher and participant interact, give us much more insight into both the study and the liturgy. Had interviewers aimed more at free associations and less at linear recall, we would have learned even more. The assumption about the relation of memory to liturgy—namely, that if liturgy is effective, it will be remembered—is one I do not buy. In any case, these dialogues tell us far more than short answers, checklists, and impressionistic quantification. Here, in section 8, we can see most clearly the values that inform the ways researchers guide those they question.

Section 9, the group interviews, could have been as valuable as the recall interviews, except it is impossible to distinguish one respondent from another. Since respondents are not named or meaningfully labeled, all the A's (Answerers, as opposed to Questioners) bleed into one another, forcing us to imagine some sort of generalized respondent. There are a few penetrating critiques of liturgy in these interviews, but there is still a great deal of posturing for the tape recorder that only a long-term study could have overcome.

What emerges from the recall and group interviews is a rhetoric of liturgical criticism that is highly generic—not specific either to ritual in general or to Catholic liturgy in particular. The ways people assess their rites—at least in the circumstances created by this study—are the same ways middle-class North Americans evaluate anything: an opera, a cafeteria, a birthday party, or a new magazine.

Consider the following list of "indigenous" terms used by participants in the study to evaluate liturgies. The list is mine, not the researchers', and items in brackets are opposites inferred from the contexts:

| *Positive* | *Negative* |
|---|---|
| active, energetic, dynamic, moving | passive [inert, static] |
| friendly, warm, welcome, at home, comfortable, personal | [distant, cold, impersonal, formalized] |
| shared | [private] |
| communal, assembly-oriented, shared | [individualistic, hierarchical, private] |
| prepared, planned | [unprepared, unplanned] |

| | |
|---|---|
| participatory | theatrical, dramatic |
| proclaimed | [merely] read |
| connectedness | formality |
| thoughtful, reflective, meaningful | habitual, rote |
| prayerful | [distracted, frivolous] |
| flowing, graceful | awkward [mechanical] |
| responsive | [flat, unanimated] |
| [innovative, unusual, special] | in a rut, ordinary |
| works | doesn't work |
| feels right or fits | doesn't feel right or fit |
| focused | [diffuse] |
| appropriate (e.g., to season or occasion) | inappropriate |
| tailor-made | generic |
| precise | [imprecise] |
| proportionate, balanced | too long, too much, too slow, too central [disproportionate] |
| serious | somber |
| festive, celebrative | serious |
| thematic [coherent] | [disjointed] |
| relevant | [dated, irrelevant] |

Lists never tell us much, but at least one can see from this one that any suspicion that there are no criteria or that they are hidden is unwarranted. The operative vocabulary is nontechnical, nontheological, not specific to liturgies as such. The same is true of the "works"/"doesn't work" distinction introduced by the researchers.[2] The actually operative criteria (as opposed to the criteria theologians think liturgists *should* used) are largely esthetic in the broad sense of the term. Only a few are explicitly religious or theological terms. Consider what terms are generally absent from the list, for example, "theologically correct," "traditional," "prescribed," "divinely revealed," "exuberant," "ornate," and the like. Their absence does not mean they are not operative—much is obviously done because it is prescribed, for example—but it does mean that such criteria are not typically negotiated in discussions.

This list of positive and negative qualities in ordinary, participant evaluation could, if studied more fully and contextually, bring to the surface some of the tensions and contradictions that lie beneath the surface. For instance, participants regularly speak of theatricality and drama as negative qualities, yet they want the Scriptures to be "proclaimed," without ever considering what such an expectation demands of one who is not in a proclamatory mood or does not have a proclamatory personality; it demands oratory, verbal dramatization. Not only are there tensions between positive and negative expectations but also between liturgical and extraliturgical values. For example, individualism and privacy seeking are bad qualities here, but most of the parishioners probably value individual initiative and creativity, own private property, and treasure their privacy at home. So one would surmise that the liturgy serves a compensatory function. When a compensatory function is operative we have learned from psychoanalysis to expect backlash. One possibility is that cultivating communal spirit in the liturgy may cause community mindedness to spill over into the larger society. But another is that having an island of communal spirit may be precisely what relieves participants' guilt for organizing the rest of their lives on the basis of individualistic, privatistic values. There is very little in the entire study that tells us how liturgies are related to social concerns such as justice, even though this is a major theme in most liturgical renewal circles.

Asked to identify the "three most troublesome things about the way the liturgy is done in your worshiping community," parishioners make generalizations: The liturgies are too long, too noisy, and too many things are happening; there is too little creativity and too much formality; the atmosphere is not warm and vibrant. Or they complain about practicalities: late arrivals, too little rehearsing, bad sound systems.

To summarize some of my major reservations about the text of the study:

- It opts for short-term survey rather than long-term field study.
- It utilizes short-answer questionnaires more often than probing interviews that pursue implications and associations.
- It assumes interviewees both can and will offer candid and penetrating critiques on the basis of questions posed by relative newcomers.

- There is no working assumption that people have unconscious motives that must be inferred from repeated observation or that people regularly dramatize themselves according to what they think interviewers want to hear.
- It assumes liturgy is experienced, recalled, and thus evaluated in terms of distinct, linear phases. Thus it tries to get at the discreet meanings of symbols rather than the sense of ritual.
- It assumes the primacy of auditory and visual sensoria and makes no systematic attempt to assess kinesthetic, gestural, and postural dimensions of liturgy. It attends primarily to the exegetical meanings of symbols (that is, what people say about those symbols), and it ignores their operational and positional meanings. For this reason crucial social contexts and issues such as those presently surrounding ethnicity, war, and gender seem to be missing from parishioners' concerns, but they, in fact, may not be.
- The study's conception of liturgical context is narrower than that of either ritual studies or the anthropology of ritual, both of which would want to know more about the social, political, geographical, ecological, and economic parameters of liturgical enactment.
- The study inquires into internal processes such as planning but never treats the planning process as inherently political as well as religious. The masters of ceremonies, homilists, and presiders do not jockey for power or compete for recognition. They do not envy one another or resent authority.

    In short, the success of the study is compromised because its aim is split between compiling data and portraying lived liturgical life. Personally, I wish it had pursued the latter. One does not have to be ridden with a penchant for debunking or hauling skeletons out of closets to argue that the study of liturgy ought to include the study of socially and physically incarnate human beings; otherwise, the liturgy will seem to float above the lived life of a congregation.

### The Rites Themselves

The grounds for liturgical assessments by outsiders obviously cannot be those of theology, liturgics, or other such disciplines of faith. But they ought not be merely private or personal. And they ought to be explicit. Mine arise from the secular discipline of religious studies generally and from ritual studies specifically. Ritual studies has been deeply influenced by symbolic anthropology and the experience of participant observation of various kinds of ritual. Since I am presently in Santa Fe on sabbatical at an anthropology center, the School of American Research, writing a book called *Ritual Criticism*, my approach to liturgical renewal reflects a cross-cultural, interreligious interest in the problem of assessing rites.

Whereas I am not hesitant to criticize studies of ritual, I walk on glass if I heed James Lopresti's advice after he read the chapter on which my presentation is based. He urged me to go beyond criticism of the text of the study to risking an assessment of the rites themselves. I have two major limitations in performing such a task: I am not a participant, and I did not observe these rites. The former can be used to disqualify my comments on religious grounds; the latter, on scholarly grounds. My only option, then, is to tender a critique of an imagined post–Vatican II liturgy based on piecemeal observations done elsewhere and on the written data before us.

Initially, I actually wrote a participant-observer's report to parallel those in the study; I called it "A Non-participant, Ignorant Observer's Report on an Imagined, Generic Post–Vatican II Liturgy." You will be relieved that I will not present that ironic, pseudovisionary ethnography here but will only summarize under three headings the desiderata that were its aftermath.

## 1. The Politics of the New Liturgy

As I sat in this imaginary parish listening to announcements delivered in an upbeat manner, I fancied the economy was still expanding; something "new" seemed to be afoot in this generic parish of Nowhere. Sitting in chairs that could be oriented toward any of the four directions and singing from Xeroxed song sheets, not hardbound hymnals: all things seemed possible there. People acted as though the house had been cleaned and it was spring, although it was really winter outside. I imagined examining the dumpsters out back to see what had been thrown away and sniffing in the closets to see what was stashed in them. How much of what has been cleaned up liturgically, I wondered, was really repressed rather than worked through? And how much of what was repressed would return?

Victor Turner, in his article "Ritual, Tribal and Catholic,"[3] bemoans the loss of the "classical" pre–Vatican II liturgy. In it he has nothing but uncritical praise for the pre–Vatican II Mass and little but disdain for the post–Vatican II version. The Mass of Pius V he considers an "architectonic masterpiece" (509), a "golden mean" (512), and, surprisingly, a bastion of liminality (524). Why he does not regard it as a veritable hyperbole of the status system he does not say. He considers the Vatican II reforms as "jaunty" revisionism and seems to imply that ritual experimentation of this sort is merely "hackwork," or worse, a dismemberment (525). The tone of his article is one of veneration for rituals that are "the work of ages" (524). He concludes it on a homiletical note: "We must not dynamite the liturgical rock of Peter" in favor of "personal religious romanticism" (526).

Though I count myself as both a friend and colleague of Vic, I flatly disagree with him. The bridges by which one might return have been burned. Nothing is to be gained by such nostalgia, though much remains to be done.

The liturgical reform was predicated on a fundamental paradigm shift that affected everything from the way worshipers attend to sensory data to ecclesiastical politics. Whenever authority is heavily invested in a hierarchy or authority figure, mystification is inherent in that process. And it was, in the old days, easy to substitute political mystification for ontological mystery. But when democratization sets in, as it has in North American liturgical renewal, it is typically accompanied by demystification. And the temptation in the demystified situation is to lapse into a managerial model with its committees, team leaders, presiders, and ministers of hospitality. However, liturgy can no more be managed democratically than it could be dictated royally or pontifically. Just as we should be suspicious of corporations when they bill themselves as their employees' "family," so we should wonder about the wisdom of speaking of huge religious bodies as "communities" or trying to make cordiality and warmth the hallmark of worship. There is a fundamental tension in my imagined contemporary parish between the rhetoric of intimacy and the scale of a multinational denomination that seems to be courting a managerial model for liturgical planning.

Accompanying the obvious tension between hierarchy and democracy is tension between structure and spontaneity. But managing spontaneity does not produce it any more than commanding it does. It is embarrassing to watch liturgists trying to generate and structure spontaneity. One has the distinct impression of a group trying too hard. The self-conscious effort undermines the very thing it is supposed to produce.

One can only wait without expectation. Spontaneity, like grace, comes in its own good time, if at all.

## 2. *The Environment and Elementals of the New Liturgy*

These "political" tensions between "royal" and "democratic" modes and between structure and spontaneity inform the esthetics and liturgics of my imagined American Catholic parish. To take a simple example, lack of screwed-to-the-floor pews in newly constructed liturgical environments suggests an incipient polydirectionality. Participants can worship facing any of the four directions. But what does this polydirectionality suggest about a group's sense of direction? If spirituality follows spatiality, and if in this case no direction is better than any other, the vertigo that results would seem to call for a kaleidoscopic liturgy. But the reformed liturgy is streamlined and comparatively linear. Environment is not ancillary to liturgy; it is generative of it. Or, at least, it ought to be. Is there a noncentripetal liturgy sufficiently polycentric to make sense out of such an environment? The loss of a unicentric sanctuary has staggering implications that parallel those attendant upon the loss of a geocentric universe. And many liturgies, I suspect, have not yet caught up to their new environments.

But how seriously does the liturgical renewal movement want to take the possibility of an environmentally integrated liturgy? Or is liturgy, by its very nature, destined always to be called indoors by the peal of a bell? Is there more than token liturgical use of nonenclosed environments, of the outdoors? Merely transporting the liturgy outside only emphasizes its disaffiliation with its own geography and climate. What would happen to a liturgy that, like the Pueblo Corn Dance, was regularly celebrated in the face of, and in concert with, the elements?

I don't know how to answer my own questions, but I believe the Vatican II liturgical reform ought to continue deepening its commitment to localization in every respect, because local knowledge is the only truly universal knowledge.

I mentioned mobile seating. Let me use another example from my imagined visit. Using freshly baked bread and homemade wine, as uncanonical as it may yet be, still goes on. Using "the real stuff" clearly signals an important recognition that taste and texture actively shape meaning—that "the elements" "under both kinds" must, in fact, be elemental. But how serious is the Church about making elemental acts and objects central? How does the removal of the Eucharist from actual feasting and ordinary eating transform its meaning? When does the elevation and stylization of the ordinary lapse into a rarification? It seems to me that the process of elementalizing, as opposed to rarification, should continue; it has much farther to go if the liturgy is to be grounded in earthen flesh, which, we are told, the Word became.

My concocted minister of hospitality pumped my hand and led me to the basement after my participant observation. There we had a "second communion," the junk-food one, and it, I am convinced, is no less real than the first one with its natural/supernatural food. Having coffee and doughnuts after bread and wine is, in my fantasy parish, a perfectly sensible but unfortunate expression of the desire for more sustained contact with things elemental in the Communion rite.

The same is true of holding hands during the Lord's Prayer, handshaking during the sign of peace, and the decorous gestures of hospitality ministers and others. As done in white, middle-class churches, these gestures strike one as self-conscious contrivances, either too intimate for groups of five hundred or too abstract to be anything other than formalized friendliness. These gestures cannot bear the load that people heap upon them. These are the gestural equivalents of the second communion—the one that transpires in the basement rather than the sanctuary. They express deep and authentic desires for sustained physical contact and social interaction, but we ought to be saddened when people speak of them as highlights of the service, just as we would be dismayed if a child said her favorite food was potato chips. Cordiality, however nice, does not nourish, and it is no substitute for spiritual connectedness, social interrelatedness, and the kinesic congruence that comes from sustained bodily engagement together. And I suspect these are more fully operative in celebrations where ethnic and gender issues are active.

### 3. The Sensorium Organization of the New Liturgy

The sensorium organization (to use Walter Ong's term) required by the liturgy has yet to be developed. I believe it must give more attention to the kinesthetic, tactile, and olfactory senses and less to visual and auditory ones if ritual knowledge is to be actually embodied. As it stands in my ignorantly observed liturgy, word and thought dominate. "Themes" are required to unify the parts, for instance, the readings and the homily. But the connections are largely intellectual. Thought out theologically, they demand to be received in the same medium. Whereas they are presented orally, they seem to imply and require pages and print to be received.

Not only do some liturgists seem inherently tied to intellectual thematizing, they seem wed to direct, didactic statement. This gives the entire liturgy, especially the Liturgy of the Word, a didactic tone, which easily suffocates the role of the arts in liturgy. Working on a very different principle from artists, liturgists are sometimes afraid to suggest lest their meaning be missed. So instead they assert and state: The homily tells us what the readings mean. In neither reading nor homily is the story felt to be sufficient unto itself. The old model of one thing's being "applied" to another still holds—in this case the homily applies the readings to life. The result is a nagging heteronomy that implies that the readings themselves are not "life" but above or beyond it. And wisdom, not to mention salvation, seems to be something that enters the ear and eye only, requiring reflection and direct action in order to be digested.

But I question the efficacy of this intellectualist, activist epistemology. The alternative posture, of which I daydreamed when I should have been taking notes on my imagined rite, is that of empty receptivity, which is best cultivated by sustained silence, practiced stillness, and kinesthetic engagement with the liturgical and ecological environment. I am not referring to the occasional addition of liturgical dance in order to enhance gospel readings. I am referring to serious meditative practice as the essential core of liturgical celebration.

What I longed for most at the end of my imagined participant observation of a post–Vatican II liturgy was sustained silence, genuine stillness, and the curvature of liturgical indirection—either this or an unthrottled exuberance, unbridled improvisation, and kinesthetic exertion. Everything I observed in my mind's eye was swift, clean, decorous, and aimed at the middle range of human emotions. The extremities were forgotten. The liturgy was cordial, friendly, open, upbeat, and more-or-less democratized. But neither God nor the world is cordial, friendly, open, upbeat, or democratized. The "scandal of Christianity" is largely displaced by such a safe, comfortable environment.

There is indeed a noble simplicity in the new liturgy; everything is up front, out in the open; nothing is hidden, nothing extra. But such an environment requires new forms of ritual knowledge, a new style of embodying mystery. Don't mistake me—I have no patience with the sort of mystification that feeds authoritarianism. But I do imagine a less self-conscious, less didactic, more suggestive liturgy. There is something about focalized attention and trying too hard that causes worshipers to miss sideways glances that feed the unconscious. And if ritual does not feed the unconscious, then ideology and advertising will. It does not require multiple altars, extended hierarchies, and an iconographic glut to evoke mystery. The simplest thing—a stone, a loaf of bread, the sound of a single water drop—is mysterious if attended to fully.

What worries me most about post–Vatican II liturgy is the kind of attention and bodily attitude it cultivates. By this I do not mean that participants cannot recall the Mass in which they have just participated. I mean that so much is aimed at eye and ear and so little at belly and foot. The liturgy, as well as the architecture and artifacts it inspires, calls upon participants to think, reflect, decide—all of which is good and necessary. But where does the worshiper have either the time or space or bodily inclination to meander in the spirit? Always erect, never on the floor, seldom in the dark, never truly hungry, never really sated, how does a people develop a physiology capable of being in the presence of a God who shakes no hands and speaks only in conundrums or in flesh?

It is tempting for the slim, trim, never-overweight Vatican II liturgy to become disembodied, because so little—beyond clumsy old pre–Vatican II buildings and ineffective sound systems—pulls it down; so little calls it to the chthonic depths. Shorn of the weight of the ages, a great deal of liturgical and architectural attention of necessity gravitates to the surfaces of things. Having opened up the Gothic closets and stripped off the baroque trim, worshipers now must attend to clean lines, ungilded surfaces, and the streamlined liturgy in which each part efficiently contributes logically and theologically to the whole. Such a liturgy requires a new quality of attention that is capable of "reading" surfaces. But who will teach this new braille, this language of the surface, this sense for the texture of meanings that are touched rather than spoken and heard? If Mother Church can become such a teacher, I will stumble over myself trying to become her first student.

### Notes

1. A more detailed treatment that demonstrates rather than states my critique of the study is included in my book, *Ritual Criticism: Case Studies in Its Practice, Essays on Its Theory* (Columbia: University of South Carolina Press, 1990).

2. The quotation marks are theirs. Although such marks indicate a recognition that the working/not working dichotomy may not be appropriate for evaluating liturgy, most of the leaders interviewed do not reject it. An exception is the Bellarmine Chapel interview summary, which concludes, ''And, the 'work/not work' format on [the] questionnaire didn't 'work.' ''

3. *Worship* 50(6) (1976) 504–526.

# Liturgy as Community Consciousness of Grace

*Roger Haight, S.J.*

**A**nyone of a certain age who grew up in the Catholic Church before the Second Vatican Council would recognize by comparison the vast differences in the whole liturgical event of the Sunday parish liturgy. A simple extended reflection on the ordinary language used to refer to Sunday worship, for example, the use of the term "liturgy" instead of "Mass," could be used to open up these differences of consciousness and practice. In the reflections that follow I will use the theology of grace as a lever to explore the status of the renewal of the liturgy in our country over the past twenty-five years. During that same period, of course, the theology of grace has also developed, and so I must begin with a somewhat extended introduction that will define the perspective on grace that will determine these reflections.

Let me begin with a definition of what I mean by the term "grace." The idea of grace is very diffuse and generalized in Scripture and in the history of theology; grace is understood in so many different ways that the word does not have a single precise content or meaning beyond the awesome and yet generic idea of God's benevolence and saving love. This is its universal significance. In order to give the term a determined meaning I shall use it to refer directly to God. I equate the symbol of grace with the biblical symbol the Spirit of God, which means God conceived as Spirit. In these reflections grace and God's Spirit are materially identical in their referent.

In the Scriptures, the Spirit of God means God, as it were, acting outside of God's self as a presence and power of life in the world. God's presence is a vitalizing and re-creating energy in the world and especially in human lives and, through them, in history.[1] Grace, then, is equivalent to the biblical notion of God's Spirit prior to its being hypostatized as a "person" or the third person of the Trinity. Economically, grace is God's Spirit or God present and at work in the lives of human beings.

The grace that is the Spirit of God has been revealed by Jesus as loving and saving. Besides being Creator God is loving Savior. Thus God, viewed now as Spirit present to and at work in human lives, is the Spirit of divine love. God loves God's creation, and the Spirit of God, or grace, is that love actively present in the lives of human beings.

This biblical notion of grace can, I believe, be neatly combined with Karl Rahner's systematic theology of grace, in which he defines grace as the self-communication of God.[2] Early in his career and in dialogue with Scholastic theology, Rahner reconceived the primacy of uncreated grace, the initiative of God's own self, over created grace, the finite effect of grace in a human being's life. By so doing he began to identify that which is referred to by grace with God's self as Spirit. More importantly, he radically personalized the notion of grace. This can be seen in two ways: first, grace *is* God's personal self; and secondly, grace is a personal communication of God's own inner self to human beings. Grace is not an impersonal power, energy, force, dynamism; grace is God's communication of God's personal self out of the depths of divine freedom.

Finally, by remaining within the Augustinian tradition of double gratuity, that is, by affirming the distinct though inseparable gratuity of God's saving self-communication in love over and above God's freedom in creation, Rahner is asserting a quasi autonomy of human existence in relation to God. God freely loves God's own creation, and human freedom can accept or reject God's offer of love. This allows human history to be conceived as an open-ended dialogue with God, a history of two freedoms. This conception integrates our experience of radical historicity with God's sovereignty over history and providential presence to it.[3]

The single most important development in the theology of grace over the past few decades finds its center in the recognition of the universality of God's offer of grace. Although this consciousness began to take shape well before Vatican II, the council's making this teaching explicit and official had revolutionary implications and consequences. Let me simply mention some of them.

The universality of grace implies a certain priority of the Spirit over Jesus in the economy of salvation.[4] The universality of grace means that the offer of God's saving Spirit is present to every single human being; grace is a gratuitous constitutive element of human existence itself. All of human history, every moment of each person's life from the beginning, unfolds within the sphere of God's being present to each in an offer of saving love. This means that no one is further from God's grace and love than any other; there is an egalitarian quality to God's gracious love. But this intuition leads with inexorable logic to the idea of the sacrality of the whole of life. The egalitarian nature of grace, if it is to be real and effective, must imply that the ordinary and most radical means for responding to God's grace consists in the everyday events that make up any given person's personal history. In sum, Vatican II's doctrine of the universality of grace implies that the very center of Christian spirituality and union with God is found, as it were, in everyday life in the world. Every other manifestation of spirituality and response to God derives from there and leads back to it.

Another development in the theology of grace since Vatican II can be seen in an interest and stress on the effectiveness of grace in terms of human life, especially social life, and history. This is especially true in the theology of Juan Luis Segundo and other liberation theologians.[5] Although not always put in these terms, this development retrieves the importance of the traditional notion of cooperative grace. Augustine defines cooperative grace as distinct from operative grace this way: "God operates . . . without us, in order that we may will [love]; but when we will [love], and so will [love] that we may act, God co-operates with us."[6] Operative grace is something that God does, as it were, to us and for us gratuitously and prior to any action of our own. Cooperative grace, which is not another grace but the follow-through of God's Spirit in human response, takes up and sustains human freedom and its action in love.

The distinction between operative and cooperative grace highlights something absolutely fundamental to the notion of grace and consequently the Christian life, namely, that they have both a passive and an active dimension. The interaction of these two dimensions, passion and action, God's action for us and human response to and with God, is central to the whole concept of grace and to Christian spirituality, and it will help to unlock much of what is going on in the dynamics of liturgy from this foundational point of view.

Let me shift now to a last aspect of the theology of grace that will be crucial for an analysis of the liturgy. Up until this point I have been speaking somewhat generally and abstractly about theological conceptions of grace apart from any experience of it. But how does grace become conscious? It may be laid down as an axiom that people can only become aware of grace through some external medium or event that bears it to explicit consciousness. This principle, which can be found in Rahner's philosophy of religion and theology of grace, flows from a general theory of knowledge that ties all knowledge to sensible data and experience of the world. This implies that all explicit or reflective consciousness of God's Spirit at work in one's life, as distinct from a vague, implicit, and unthematic consciousness of it, must be mediated through historical events. For Christians, the event and whole life of Jesus constitute the primary tangible historical symbol, which identifies and objectifies for consciousness the content of the inner working of God's Spirit, or grace. This foundational axiom may be looked upon as the sacramental principle that will have a direct bearing on all liturgical practice.

Much more could be said about the theology of grace. But these fundamental principles are enough to define the point of view operating in these reflections as well as their *status quaestionis.* The issue addressed here concerns the way liturgy functions in the history of grace within the Christian community. More concretely and in the light of the data of liturgical practice in the United States, how is liturgy actually mediating grace?

The method underlying these reflections on the praxis of liturgy will consist in a kind of dialogue between an a priori understanding of grace provided by the theology of grace and the data of the descriptions of actual liturgical practice that have been provided by the organizers of this conference. In this dialogue I began with the data of actual liturgies and made generalizations appropriate to the theology of grace. But in the interests of an orderly presentation I shall for the most part begin from principles from the theology of grace and either find them exemplified or concretized in the data or use them to critically reflect on the significance of the data. Although the goal here is to measure the distance covered since Vatican II, I shall not use the obvious method of comparing liturgy now with liturgy before the council but shall remain within the context of a dialogue between a current theology of grace and present-day liturgical practice. The primary focus of these reflections is always the Eucharistic liturgy.

These reflections are divided into four general areas of reflection, each one of which is introduced by a summary thesis or proposition that summarizes a general principle or conclusion about the liturgy.

These particular theses have not been arrived at on an a priori basis, although I believe they articulate general truths. They have been dictated by reflection on the descriptive data provided by the research into the actual liturgical practice of the fifteen parishes in the United States. Thus, when taken together, they are not meant to purvey a single or unified conclusion.

### 1. The Nature of Liturgy

We begin with a thesis on the nature of liturgy that flows from the theology of grace and is borne out by the actual practice of liturgy today: Liturgy is a graced assembly; people bring grace to the assembly.

This view is general; it could also apply to the liturgies of other religions and even to some nonexplicitly religious gatherings. In its first moment, liturgy may be defined as a coming together of people, as an actual assembly, as the event of coming together. In Christian liturgy, this assembly is graced in the sense that it is convoked on the basis of the impetus of a religious experience of God's Spirit in the lives of those who come together. The real point of the thesis is the recognition that concretely and historically it is the participants themselves who, as it were, "bring grace" to the liturgy from the world of their daily lives.[7]

This conception of liturgy and the grace it bears may be called a view "from below." It should not, however, be seen as an attack on the initiative of God in every performance of the liturgy. The point is neither to deny the objective quality of liturgy nor the dimension of the priority of this celebration to each one of its participants as individuals. This objective quality is derived from the liturgy's foundation in the external life of Jesus and its long tradition in the Christian community. The point made here is meant to complement this objectivity by a concrete existential and historical point of view. The reality of the liturgy is constituted by the event of a community assembling in this place here and now. All are familiar with the principle in sacramental theology that the Church is the primary and grounding sacrament of the other particular sacraments. Extending this to liturgy, one should conceive the actual gathering of people together, that is, Church actualized, as the primary sacrament that the liturgy itself is.

The idea of people bringing grace to the liturgy flows from the conviction of the universality of grace. The grace that is God's loving and saving Spirit is universally abroad, and it is prior to and more basic than any liturgy or even any self-conscious awareness of it. The priority of grace, its gratuitous and a priori character relative to human existence itself and all aspects of concrete life, means that those who are impelled to liturgical worship are already cooperating with the impulses of grace in their lives. The primary and, as it were, subterranean locus of God's gracious presence to people in the liturgy then comes through people themselves as they assemble. People bring to one another a renewal of grace within the context of their explicit Christian faith.

There are many indications that this consciousness is implicitly or explicitly at work in the various communities whose liturgies have been described for us. In what follows I will point out some aspects of the liturgies celebrated across the United States that help to define concretely the significance of the general proposition. In a way, these qualities of the liturgies define concretely the meaning of the generalized formula.

One piece of data from which the thesis may be inferred is the emphasis on "welcoming" as a distinct component of the liturgy itself. Ushers have consciously become ministers of hospitality. But not only these ministers; all the participants can themselves share this ministry of hospitality by welcoming others. The silent preparation for Mass has yielded to a conscious and often vocal gathering of a community; everyone, including the celebrant, becomes involved in constituting the body that will perform liturgy.[8] There are, of course, many intentionalities at work in these new practices. But from a theological perspective one has to be a recognition of any and every person, even the outside visitor, as one whose being and value are defined by his or her being an object, subject, and bearer of God's grace.

Another strong indication of a new awareness of this truth appears in the strongest and most commonly appreciated value attached to the renewed liturgy, namely, the active participation that it has engendered among those who assemble for it. Over and over again both the liturgical teams, the people who assume designated liturgical ministries, and those among the assembled body witness to their own sense of participation and that of others. This participation implies ownership, being a part of something that is not simply other and out there for the spectator. The enactment in voice and movement of the liturgy, and even in corporate silence, gives expression to an experience of God's Spirit within each and within the assembly itself.

The idea that liturgy is a graced assembly in which the participants create the common expression of the encounter with God's Spirit is also reflected in the careful planning that goes into every Sunday liturgy. This planning presupposes an appreciation of the "event quality" of each celebration. This event quality, in its turn, must be carefully balanced over against the stable structure of Roman Catholic liturgy, which also has its value. As one reflector insightfully puts it, if each liturgy were not in some degree routinized but were created anew each time, it would not release the human spirit into prayer. Participants would be constantly preoccupied by what was coming next. Yet this routine structure in all the liturgies sampled has remained precisely that, a structure, and not a merely objective formula for a mechanical series of events. The consciousness implied in this planning may be described as a recognition of the existentially unique quality of each liturgy as an event, an event in which all the participants participate in and through the Spirit of God active at this moment within them.

A final indication of the existential nature of the liturgy, such that the graced participants constitute the liturgy itself, is displayed in the enculturation and adaptation that has occurred in the American implementation of it. A superficial review of the various liturgies, just as an inattentive assistance at the liturgy in a variety of parishes, could engender an experience of sameness. They all have the same basic structure; variations are, relatively speaking, minute when compared with the essential pattern. But nothing could be further from the truth. Each of the liturgies express a great many of the concrete variables that constitute each community: region, race, culture, social identity, economic background and class, ethnic identity, not to mention the physical determinants of climate and space. This extraordinary individualization of each community's liturgy within the still rather rigid stable structure demonstrates, I think, the thesis that the most fundamental nature of the liturgy should be looked upon as the community assembled itself in its act of assembling.

The significance of this first reflection on liturgy from the point of view of the theology of grace stands out in opposition to an excessive stress on its opposite, an objectivist understanding of *the* liturgy, as if the liturgy existed in objective fashion before it is performed. An overly objective understanding of the liturgy would reduce participants to passive receivers of something that they did not already possess, namely, God's loving grace in the form of God's self-communicating Spirit. Fundamentally, the action of liturgy is the opposite of that. It is people, who already live in the sphere of God's Spirit because God's Spirit lives in them, coming together and performing liturgy. People gathering and gathered are the historical event of the sacrament. In and by their coming together they intensify or communicate to each other in a new way an experience of grace in their lives.

This understanding of the liturgy also defines the intrinsic continuity between liturgy and life in the world of history, society, and daily affairs. The grace mediated in and through liturgy is not "another grace." There is absolutely nothing new or special about the liturgy, ontologically speaking, that can be added to the very gift of God's own self to human beings. God's Spirit is a constant and intrinsically present element of daily life, and the response to grace is mediated by human responses to the situations and people that make up the ordinary events of life. This continuity helps to clarify the reality of liturgy. Liturgy, too, is a this-worldly event in the history of Christian life, along with all the others, but one that explicitly draws upon life's deepest sacral and constitutive element, namely, God's being present to human existence as personal love and involvement.

## 2. *The Immediate Purpose of Liturgy*

What is the fundamental point of liturgy? Why does the Christian community come together and celebrate liturgy in a public way? A response to this question can be formulated in another thesis that arises out of the data of the actual celebrations of liturgy across the country. The immediate purpose of liturgy is to bring grace to conscious expression, and this occurs in a great variety of ways.

Several aspects of a contemporary theology of grace point to the conclusion that the immediate purpose of liturgy is not to cause or confer grace where it does not exist. We have already spoken of the priority of grace to the liturgy on the basis of its priority to human existence itself. All people live in a sphere of grace, and the only authentic impulse that would impel one to liturgy would be the movement of and response to God's Spirit. Moreover, once grace is conceived in personalist categories as God's communication of God's self, engendering a free personal response out of freedom, the result is a conception of union with God primarily in interpersonal terms. Such a personal self-communication of God cannot be thought of in quantitative terms of more or less; grace cannot be reified. But one can speak of degrees of the intensity of one's response to God. People, then, do not "bring grace" to the liturgy in order to confer it on one another. Rather, a response to grace is intensified by its communal coming to expression in liturgical celebration.

The liturgies surveyed from across the country show that this bringing of grace to expression in a conscious way occurs in an extraordinary variety of ways. The differences here, I believe, may be related to the variables responsible for the enculturation and adaptation mentioned earlier. Of course, there is a deep structure to Christian Eucharistic liturgy that remains constant; it finds its center in the memory of Jesus' life, death, and resurrection and thus brings to expression the paschal mystery, which defines the deepest God-given structure of human existence itself. The fundamental realities of life and death, the paradoxical paradigm of life through death and resurrection, constitute the deepest mystery of God and human existence revealed in Jesus. This paschal mystery gives substance, form, and content to the experience of God's Spirit as grace.

But this fundamental and substantial content that comes to expression in Eucharistic liturgy finds all sorts of derivative and multifaceted expressions of God's self-communication in the distinct parts of the liturgy. It is fascinating to see how many different elements of the liturgy are considered the high points or the crucial moments in the accomplishment of the liturgy's immediate purpose. A simple enumeration of some of these from the testimony of both those planning the liturgies and those participating in them will be instructive.

For some the high point of the liturgy is Communion. This experience is probably the one that is most consistent with a traditional, in the sense of pre–Vatican II, experience of the Mass. But for others the communal reciting or singing of the Lord's Prayer and the gesture of peace is the high point of the liturgy. Here, more than at any moment in the ritual action, one can experience a sense of solidarity and actual community in an existential sense. This is consistent with a conception of Eucharistic liturgy whose purpose is to express and build a sense of an actual community of commonly shared and nurtured faith.

In other practices or experiences of the liturgy the homily has assumed a kind of centrality within the whole. For the homily makes explicit sense out of the whole; it represents a coming to explicit consciousness of the meaning of the celebration itself by means of a statement of direct address to the community in prose form, and the relating of it to the lives of the participants. Some people await the sermon as the key moment, allow it to color the rest of the ritual action, and then carry it with them beyond the liturgy into their lives.

For still others, music makes the liturgy; so important has this become that some might declare, "no music, no liturgy." One can think of very many rationales that would support this view beyond the practical facts of the matter. Music and song are perhaps the most intense and attractive ways of bringing religious experience to expression. In the end, one finds it difficult to argue with the concrete fact that the success of many liturgies clearly rests on the foundations of music and choir.

Still another aspect of liturgy that has arisen as a central element of the Eucharist lies in the more diffuse experience that what makes the liturgy is the sheer coming together of the community. This is reflected in the attention given to the two extremes of the community's assembling; the informal gathering before it and the attention given in some communities to gathering after it through such practices as coffee hours and other forms of social gathering. In some communities these are no longer really the before and after of the liturgy but parts of it, once again highlighting the recognition that the nature of liturgy at its most fundamental level is the gathering of the community.

Is there something to be learned from this variety of data concerning the many different ways in which the immediate purpose of the liturgy is realized? It seems to me that this data ratifies the existential and historical-event quality of Eucharistic liturgy. Liturgy is a series of events that together make up a whole. This way of thinking about liturgy may explain the lack of the word "sacrament" in the dossiers, and perhaps also the lack of a professional sacramental theologian in these proceedings. In many ways the Eucharistic Prayer and certainly the consecration have been dethroned as the center of Eucharistic liturgy. This should not, I repeat, be understood as a negation of the deep objective structure that underlies the Eucharistic liturgy. But this structure is the underpinning of an existential event. No element within the actual unfolding of events is considered the core sacrament. Rather, the whole of the liturgical proceedings with the great diversity of its discrete elements or parts is the sacrament. Any one of the parts can bring to consciousness the whole deep structure of the paschal mystery.

In sum, this then is the immediate purpose of Eucharist: to bring to a new, explicit, and intensified consciousness the reality of the grace that forms the context of human life, which Christians, along with all others, already bear within themselves as God's Spirit of love. In daily life any event or thing encountered in the world can become an occasion for a conscious realization or experience of this grace. Liturgy is the community's ritual event whose purpose is to consciously recall and intensify this experience. Any element within the course of the liturgy itself may become central for different persons or groups at any given time.

### 3. *The Passive and Active Dimensions of Eucharist*

The data of the dossiers describing the liturgies throughout the United States reflect the pattern of the dynamics of grace. These liturgies have a passive and an active dimension. The liturgies symbolize the priority of God's love and forgiveness; they also provide a stimulus or challenge in leading the Christian life. In terms of human response, these dimensions of the liturgy reflect an acceptance of God's gratuitous initiative in grace and the active response that acceptance of grace entails.

The passive dimension in the dynamics of grace corresponds to the total gratuity of God's love and the complete priority of God's initiative to human response. This theme of the gratuity of grace is universal beneath all the different conceptions of grace in the history of Christian theology. This gratuity is reflected in Augustine's term "operative grace" that was explained at the outset of this paper. By contrast, "cooperative grace" points to the active side of the response to grace. Grace is always prior, but God's presence impels or opens up and draws out of itself the human spirit in self-transcending love.

It is not by accident that these two fundamental dimensions in the dynamics of grace are echoed in the liturgy. It may be useful to highlight those elements of the liturgy that reflect each side of the tension. The passive elements of the liturgy are those that express acceptance and gratitude for what God has and is doing for human existence. One acknowledges sin and accepts God's forgiveness in the *Kyrie*. The Eucharistic Prayer, the Lord's Prayer, the gesture of peace, Communion, all reflect this passive dimension of the liturgy, for they commemorate what God has done in the community. Periods of silence in the liturgy, often neglected, can be a vehicle for arousing the experience or response of acceptance of God's action in one's life and the life of the community. The very assembly, the community itself and the socializing that is its reality, is something that is received in a faith that is caused by the initiative of God's Spirit.

What I have been calling the passive dimension in the dynamics of grace obviously does not imply that liturgy is mute or inactive. I simply mean that the primary theme in this response is marked by pure gratitude, praise, and acceptance. A pointed example of this can be seen in the *Kyrie*. More than once in the reflective accounts of the liturgies the *Kyrie* seems to break the rhythm of the initial entrance, the theme of joy in the song preceding the opening rites. The mood of celebration seems to be cut short. While the words of the *Kyrie* lead in this direction by pleading for forgiveness, and while the recollection and self-accusation of sin is especially somber, the theology of the dynamics of grace do not support this mood. For, as was said at the outset, one does not come to the liturgy without God's forgiving grace. The revelation of God in Jesus is quite clear that all human beings are already forgiven prior to anything that they might do on their own behalf. In fact, then, what is going on in the *Kyrie* should be an expression of joy and celebration that one has already been forgiven. The theology of grace does not recommend a triumphalist celebration free from a self-knowledge of our sinful selves. Indeed, sin defines another existential structure of human existence. But the grace of having already been accepted by God's love even with our sin is one of the most profound and joyous of radical Christian experiences. The "passive" response to it should be one of sheer gratitude.[9] Somehow the subtlety of this theme ought to be able to be brought to artistic expression, especially in music.

The active dimension of the liturgy, it seems to me, is most clearly concentrated in the Liturgy of the Word and the homily. There is no need here to rehearse all the historical reasons that have led to a retrieval of this crucial aspect of the liturgy. In theological terms, the Word identifies the Spirit; Jesus is the norm and criterion for what is authentically the Spirit of God; Scripture provides the lens through which one discovers and interprets the Spirit active in everyday life. The deep structure of the liturgy is *memoria Jesu*, a recalling and bringing forward of the central historical symbol that structures Christian faith. The homily, then, bears in explicit terms the very meaning of the symbolic events of ritual. Obviously the homily should carry both the passive and the active dimension of the liturgy, since the active dimension is impossible without the passive. But let me dwell for a moment on how the homily is especially suited to carrying the active dimension.

Many of the reflections on the homily both by planners and participants use the term "challenging." A good homily is one that intersects with the actual lives of the congregation and challenges them to the demands of grace. The homily calls forth the human ideals contained in the Scriptures and presents Jesus as the norm of Christian life. Ultimately it is Jesus who becomes the criterion for identifying the authentic direction of the movement of God's Spirit. But there are two different ways of reading the New Testament stories about Jesus and representing their meaning to the congregation, one corresponding to the passive dimension of the dynamics of grace, the other to the active component.

In the passive mode, one looks at and relates to Jesus as the medium of God's salvation for human beings and for each one of us. Each person in the congregation is the beneficiary of God's salvation mediated by and identified in Jesus. From the active side of the dynamics of grace, however, one reads the stories of Jesus as a disciple. Here, one does not look at Jesus so much as a beneficiary of Jesus' life or as a recipient of the salvation mediated through him, although this is not excluded, but one identifies with Jesus. When the Christian puts himself or herself in the place of Jesus in a story about him, the whole tenor and meaning is shifted to one of responsibility and challenge. This is the spirituality of the *imitatio Christi*, of discipleship. Within the context of faith in Jesus, the Spirit of God impels one to look closely at the humanity of Jesus, to take on his values as one's own, and to act as Jesus acted. I will say more about this in the thesis that follows.

To summarize this section, I have simply tried to show how the liturgy as it is actually experienced today recapitulates the elementary polarity of the dynamics of the interaction between God and human existence that is formulated in the theology of grace. The theology of grace at this point is absolutely elementary; we are dealing here with God's contact with human existence as Spirit and how human beings respond to and are united with God. These passive and active dimensions are just that, dimensions of a dynamic interpersonal relation that cannot be separated. They flow into and feed each other. So too is the liturgy a single event of the congregated community. But its many facets and elements bear specific thematic qualities that should be reflected upon, kept in balance, and emphasized according to the needs of the community at any particular time. Sometimes the passive dimension may need emphasis; at other times the active may need to be stressed. But always both dimensions should be present.

### 4. The Goal of Liturgy

A fourth general statement about the liturgy can be seen arising out of the dialogue between actual practice and the theology of grace: the goal of liturgy may be defined as animating Christian life in the world.

What was referred to earlier as the immediate purpose of liturgy may be distinguished from its broader goal. Earlier, it was shown from the theology of grace that God's Spirit is universally operative, so that the grace mediated in liturgy is really already encountered in everyday life. People bring grace to the assembly in order that it may come to explicit consciousness in celebration. But it is not sufficient to maintain that celebration is an end in itself. It is true that there is a certain givenness and gratuity in worship that seems to allow one to dwell in it without consideration of further ends or consequences. But ultimately this is a shortsighted view that short-circuits the dynamics of grace and the will of God for the Christian life. For it is rare in our Scriptures that God is presented as desirous of worship for its or God's own sake. Quite on the contrary, the Scriptures are laden with practical moral considerations that betray a divine utilitarianism. It is not the person who says "Lord, Lord" who enters into God's kingdom, but the one who does the will of the heavenly Father.[10]

Liturgy, then, can be seen as a center of a larger, circular movement that is animated by the Spirit of God brought "from the world" by the participants to the celebration and whose comprehensive goal is to lead to a grace-inspired life in the world. This should be conceived without dualisms, without any view of a world devoid of grace as opposed to the religious sphere filled with it. Rather, in the liturgy the grace of the world becomes conscious in memory and promise in order that it may become intensified in daily life. When one views the liturgy not simply in itself but within the context of the whole Christian life, one cannot, I think, come to another conclusion.

There is no doubt that the concerns of the world are heavy on the minds of the people who participate in the liturgy. Time and again in the recollections of those who assisted at the liturgies surveyed, participants recall their preoccupation at any given time with concerns from their daily lives. Often these are focused in crises in which they or other people find themselves. Moreover, at two junctures in the liturgy this all-encompassing goal of the liturgy becomes the focus of attention. The first is the general intercessions in which the needs of the world, largely secular in nature, are placed before God. People are asked to draw into their consciousness the larger context of life itself, our secular history and common venture as a human race in this world, to be laid at the altar before God. Indeed, each particular liturgy is meant to be a kind of liturgy of the world.

The other moment where the daily concerns of Christian life in the world come to the forefront is the homily. I have already described the importance from the point of view of the theology of grace for the homily to have two dimensions, passive and active, corresponding to operative and cooperative grace. The homily should reflect on the priority of God as loving forgiveness and the source of comfort and reconciliation; it should also challenge, not by threat but by opening up new possibilities in life by the power of grace. In most of the descriptions of the liturgies, the formula for such a homily is referred to in two steps as, first, explaining the readings, and, secondly, applying their meaning to daily life. So standard is this view that one might suspect that it may have been provided by the language of the survey itself.

I would like to suggest that there may be inherent difficulties with this formula, as innocent as it sounds. First, it is difficult to simply begin by explaining the meaning of the readings, as it were, in a vacuum. As familiar as the texts of the Gospels may be, they still come from a distant time and place that are culturally quite alien to our own situation. They need an interpretative key to unlock their simple yet profound meaning, which has its basis in common human religious experience. Secondly, although no one follows such a formula slavishly, by itself it tends toward a kind of moralistic reduction of the meaning of the Scriptures. The payoff of the homily should not be moralistic but the opening up of the religious meaning of the Gospel.

A simple way of avoiding these possible difficulties is to reverse the formula, to begin first of all with daily life, and then, secondly, to interpret the Scriptures in the light of the existential and social questions that description of our contemporary experience raises to the surface. In fact, this is really the mental mechanism that underlies the actual construction of a homily even under the previous formula. The Scriptures were written by people who had basic human religious needs and questions that arose out of their lives. To even begin to understand them, one has to raise the same kind of questions from within the experience of ourselves today. Everyone's life today is in some way stymied, personally and socially; negativities press in at all levels; these give rise to and are the impetus behind all religious questioning. For *the* religious question is the question of salvation. Only on the basis of this question, or these questions, can Scripture be intelligible as providing some saving response.

The payoff of the homily, then, is not moralistic. It is rather a new understanding of grace, of God's Spirit in one's life as witnessed to and clarified by the Scriptures. It is a recognition of a new power in daily human life and a recognition of new possibilities, new beginnings, re-creation. Challenge is not provided by moral exhortation but by an encounter with a *kairos* or opportunity for a new kind of behavior in the everyday dilemmas of existence that is provided by the power of God's values and God's Spirit.

Let me try to summarize in more general terms the point of this last proposition concerning the liturgy from the point of view of the theology of grace. The definition of the goal of the liturgy as animating Christian life in the world implies what might be called the historical efficacy of liturgical celebration. The importance of this view, I believe, lies in its contrast to a certain tendency to view the liturgy exclusively as an event in and of itself. Without attempting to deny the need for this specialization or that liturgy is a discrete datum of the Christian life, one must also see it in the broader context of the liturgy of life itself, the great drama that we as individuals, but especially as a group and as members of the human race, act out in the time allotted us. In this grander context, liturgy is but a part, albeit a crucial and necessary part of the Christian life. The historical efficacy of the liturgy should not be understood in crude instrumental and manipulative categories. It finds its basis in the very Spirit of God, God's self-communication in grace, which underlies the whole of human existence and every single aspect of daily life as a call to self-transcendence in love. Operative grace must lead to cooperative grace. What is celebrated in liturgy is real and actual because and in the measure that it becomes actualized in the concrete living of the values of the gospel outside of the liturgy, or, within the liturgy of the world. The goal of Sunday liturgy, then, its point, is this efficacy, the making real in history of the grace that one has experienced and appropriated in the liturgical celebration.

## Conclusion: New Developments

Let me briefly summarize the theological proposals that have been made in the course of these reflections. These propositions have been impelled from the standpoint of the theology of grace, whose scope extends well beyond that of liturgy. But they are not proposed in abstraction from the data of the parishes we are considering. Rather, they have emerged out of a dialogue and thus have been found to be implicit in the descriptions and evaluations of the liturgies proposed for our consideration.

One can define liturgy not only existentially, historically, and descriptively but also theologically as the actual assembly of Christians. Some theologians see in the worshiping community assembled the very definition of the Church. Thus, Church, from one point of view, is not prior to its members assembled; liturgy is not grace possessed and offered by an objective agency to its members. People bring grace to the liturgy, and this gives a theological rational to the themes of participation and communitarian interchange that are highlighted in these dossiers. This view maximizes the importance of conscious planning of each liturgy and of stimulating a sense of corporate responsibility for it and participation in it.

The immediate purpose of liturgy is to bring to consciousness in a communitarian way the experience of grace, which is the very basis of faith. What is striking about the data is the extraordinary variety of ways in which this actually occurs. All the parts of the whole liturgy, each with its specific theme, may assume a great importance for this or that person or for this community as opposed to another. Seeing the liturgy not as an entity but as a series of events making up a whole, a drama in which each element shares an importance all its own, yet not detached from the others, has enabled an adaptation and enculturation that is one of the great achievements of the developments since Vatican II.

The structure of the dynamics of God's Spirit in human life, characterized as the tension between passion and action, reception and active response, finds its correlate in the dynamics of the liturgy. Neither should predominate, neither should be exclusively emphasized. The interaction of what we have received from God and our new freedom and responsibility in grace should be orchestrated to feed and increase each other.

Finally, liturgy must also be considered in the wider context of Christian life in the world. The larger purpose or goal of liturgy is to animate Christian life in the world. But this should not engender a crass instrumental construct of how this goal is to be achieved. Liturgy is the very opposite of moralistic exhortation, of imposing obligations on human freedom. Liturgical purposiveness is religious; it seeks to open up to religious exigency and imagination a new way of life that can be empowered by God's Spirit alive in the world.

I would like to conclude these reflections on the data of liturgical celebration around the country by pointing to some new developments that appear on the horizon. For the most part the focus of these remarks has been exclusively on the present practice of the liturgy. Only by implicit contrast have they included any reference to the way things were done before the Second Vatican Council. There has been no need, I think, to state the obvious distance that liturgy has traveled in twenty-five years. But the point of this conference would be minimized if it only reveled in the new vitality of our worshiping communities. Continued development is latent in the data of the liturgies, and one can only expect continued enculturation and adaptation to our surrounding world, society, and Church. I believe that one can see some of the future, if only in vague general terms, in response to new exigencies, reflected in the very language used to describe liturgy as it is practiced today. This will become clear, I think, against the horizon of movements that are presently at work within society and the Church.

One thing a reader of the dossiers could hardly miss is the relative infrequency of the word "priest." The leader of Sunday worship is called the "presider" or "celebrant." Shifts of language such as this necessarily carry with them a shift of consciousness and understanding. The principal role of presider is to preside, to lead, and the success of the presider is judged existentially by this ability to function as a leader within this worshiping community. The language and practices of general participation, especially in the variety of responsible ministerial roles beyond that of presiding, also contain impulses for development. Also striking is the various responsibilities that women have assumed in the actual working of the whole liturgical celebration. When these data are viewed against the background of the actual historical situation of a great many communities deprived of the Eucharist, and of the movement of women in society and in the Church, one has to have a sense that new developments are taking place right within these data themselves. It is very difficult to isolate causes of historical development, for the reasons for changes in historical situations and for the emergence of a new consciousness in communities are always multiple and complex. Yet I believe the values and ideals reflected in these liturgies are the seeds for changes in the criteria for ordination. These changes, which will change again the liturgy itself, have to occur for the values and ideas that are celebrated in the liturgy to be credibly witnessed to and celebrated.

The same values of participation and building community in existential terms point to another development. There is a point where the size of a church or the gathered congregation begins to militate against realizing these values on a regular basis. Thus, there is an exigency internal to the dynamics of these liturgies themselves toward a breakdown of those enormous Sunday Masses in which the interpersonal and communitarian ideal cannot be nurtured. Again, this internal dynamic can be measured against the horizon of the movement of Basic Ecclesial Communities, which has spread beyond Latin America. Of course, this development too has an uneven application. Rural churches, and in some cases established suburban congregations, may share many of the characteristics of basic communities. The dossiers manifest this. But large urban parishes may not be able to minister liturgically to great numbers of Catholics in the same way, and many people will find a more vital kind of worship in smaller, non-Catholic Churches. The data of the liturgies that we have considered exemplify a large degree of social and cultural adaptation. As this enculturation continues, especially in areas where there is a large concentration of Catholics, the values of participation, community, and leadership arising out of the community should move in the direction of more basic communities within large parishes and toward more expansive, less exclusive criteria for leadership within the liturgical community than the norm of celibate males allows.

### Notes

1. John L. McKenzie, "Aspects of Old Testament Thought," *Jerome Biblical Commentary*, ed. R. Brown, J. Fitzmyer, and R. Murphy (Englewood Cliffs, N.J.: Prentice Hall, 1968) 742.

2. "Grace, Theological," *Encyclopedia of Theology: The Concise* Sacramentum Mundi, ed. Karl Rahner (New York: Seabury, 1975) 589–591.

3. See George Vandervelde, "The Grammar of Grace: Karl Rahner as a Watershed in Contemporary Theology," *Theological Studies* 49 (1988) 445–459, for a lucid analysis of the fundamental logic of Rahner's theology of grace.

4. This point needs considerably more reflection and qualification than can be given here.

5. See Juan Luis Segundo, *Grace and the Human Condition*, trans. John Drury (Maryknoll, N.Y.: Orbis Books, 1973); relative to the liturgy, see especially *Sacraments Today*, trans. John Drury (Maryknoll, N.Y.: Orbis Books, 1974).

6. "On Grace and Free Will," *Basic Writings of Saint Augustine*, 1, ed. Whitney J. Oates (New York: Random House, 1948) 761.

7. This point, although explored in the context of a different problematic, is developed by Karl Rahner in "Considerations on the Active Role of the Person in the Sacramental Event," *Theological Investigations* 14 (New York: Seabury, 1976) 161–184.

8. I am indebted to David Rankin, S.J., an Australian liturgist, for this particular reflection and for several other refinements of the argument of this paper.

9. This theme in the history of the theology of grace is probably best expressed by Martin Luther. See, for example, his *Freedom of the Christian,* in *Luther's Works,* 31, ed. Harold J. Grimm (Philadelphia: Muhlenberg Press, 1957) 327–377.

10. This is most dramatically portrayed in the prophetic writings and in the Gospels when Jesus is seen in the role of a prophet announcing that God's cause is the cause of human existence. Cf. Edward Schillebeeckx, *Jesus: An Experiment in Christology,* trans. Hubert Hoskins (New York: Vintage Books, 1981) 229.

# A Response to the Study from the Standpoint of Christology

*Gerard S. Sloyan*

**My** remarks will have to do chiefly with the Church's Christological doctrine as it is promulgated and received in the Catholic West. Although theoretically this teaching is identical with that of the Catholic East, it is not given the same expression in the Eastern Rites, either as regards ritual or text. Similarly, the heartlands of Catholic Eastern faith and practice have different political experiences from those of the West and the places evangelized by it, especially the Southern Hemisphere. And Christologies are forged by political experiences. The case can be made, of course, that in cultures like those of the United States and Canada, realities that have influenced Christological perception such as gender, race, ethnicity, and class are largely homogeneous, as between Catholics of the Roman, the one surviving Western Rite, and the several Eastern Rites.

It will not be easy to comment on the study from the standpoint of the Church's Christological faith because there are not sufficient indications within it of how that faith is understood, professed, and lived, to do so. That itself may be indicative. But this should not be taken as a criticism of the study which is already sufficiently ingenious, concentrating as it does on modes of celebration and reactions to them by parishioners, liturgical ministers, and skilled facilitators of these liturgies. At times, the Christology of the interviewers is discernible, as when one of them reminds a person in a group interview of a time when they had been in a graduate class together, a class that had done much renovation of the sanctuary and had "ignored the primary symbol of Christ, the assembly itself." That is a pertinent Christological comment, no less than it is ecclesial. Its content is found more than once, as expressed by parish directors of liturgy and priest-presiders. One has the net impression that participants in the study are aware, through their conduct as much as what they say, that the glorified, heavenly Christ is the whole Christ, his body on earth as a people at prayer and work and—for the fortunate—at play. But this is an impression one derives. It is hard to document by specific citations from the study. Similarly, when one hears mention of a hymn entitled "Gentle Shepherd," one recognizes the Christological title immediately. Ezekiel, Luke, and John all have such a concept of God or Christ as shepherd, although they may not use the precise word. A tracking down of the words of the hymn would indicate the Christology of the lyricist and, by extension, of those who choose and those who appreciate the song. But extrapolating from the few pieces of data I have cited and from others like them scattered throughout the study could be a risky business. I hesitate to engage in it.

We do not have a record of the Christological convictions of the presiders, the homilists, or the directors of liturgy and of music of these fifteen congregations. We might be able to conclude much from such documentation. It is clear that they all view the Lord's Supper much as Saint Paul did and some in the Corinthian congregation did not: as a living symbol of the harmony that should prevail in the body. That body is one that individuals can be guilty of violating if they do not examine themselves sufficiently before they eat and drink. The body must be distinguished, discerned, for what it is if eating the bread and drinking the cup of the Lord unworthily is not to bring judgment in condemnation (see 1 Cor 11:27-29). That sense of the corporate Christ, the "entire redeemed city" of Saint Augustine's thought (*De civitate Dei* 10, 6), is very clear from the comments of all participants in the study. What we do not have is a clear picture of who Jesus Christ is thought to be in himself and, more importantly, who he is for us, for the worshipers, on the basis of the survey. One can assume that he is the congregants' life, their light, the high priest who offered the acceptable sacrifice of himself once for all and pleads for us beyond the veil of the heavens, the sympathetic figure of Hebrews who "is not ashamed to call us his siblings" (2:11), or "the Son of man who will come on a cloud with great power and glory," of the Lucan gospel (21:27). One can further assume that the worshipers believe him to be one in being with the Father and a human being born of a virgin, Mary, as some (but not all) of the fifteen congregations profess verbally each Sunday.

An exit poll of the participating congregations would probably not disclose much about their Christological beliefs. It might well yield the remembered conciliar and catechism response that Jesus Christ is "true God and true man." That answer would be likely to come from the best and the worst of regular worship situations equally, telling us little of the quality of the worship and how it formed people's views. Catholics do not express their faith well in words. Even after twenty-one ecumenical councils and the sunderings of the eleventh and sixteenth centuries, they have not become accustomed to expounding it clearly upon challenge. The extended interviews bear that out. The best educated among those interviewed tend to speak anecdotally of the faith they hold, not at all in biblical or doctrinal terms. A simple person in one of the parishes speaks beautifully of sitting in the church alone one day, thinking of the time his father sat there—and there—and there—in the church, and of all the people of the parish who are now out in the churchyard. It is a marvelous testimony to faith in the communion of saints, which is probably not what *hē koinōnia tōn hagiōn/communio sanctorum* meant to those who coined the creedal phrase! My point is that clear Christological phrasing may not have been available to many in the survey besides the preachers, who by a duty of state have to put the Church's faith into words. One can only hope that they and all homilists do this regularly.

Would the Christology of these worshipers, once elicited from them, prove to be of the popular Monophysite kind that prevails in all the Churches, Roman Catholic, Orthodox, Protestant, and fundamentalist—doctrinally correct but barely? I think not, from the few hints the survey provides. I think that their faith is better than that. These people are hearing and singing from week to week in the liturgical texts that Jesus is Lord and Christ, the Word of God and the Son of God; but also that he is one of us, flesh of our flesh and bone of our bone, a suffering human being like the rest of us. His origins in the Godhead as Word are not for them an ocean in which the drop of honey of his humanity is drowned.

Eutyches may have lost the battle at Chalcedon, but he certainly won the war. In this he had the powerful backing of Cyril, who proved orthodox by a Chalcedonian standard—he was dead seven years when it met—orthodox by a hair. Cyril lives long in the Church's memory for having maintained subtly what the old monk Eutyches maintained crudely, that the one hypostasis of the Word prevails, predominates, in the union of natures. Nestorius, meantime, is recalled in infamy as the author of a heresy he probably did not profess. For the "two-natures" people of Antioch had to be described constantly as "two-persons" people by Alexandria if the unity and indivisibility of the person of the Word was to be maintained.

You know how it ended. A letter of a Western bishop, Leo, in Rome, to Flavian, his fellow patriarch in Constantinople, won the day. Its theology was largely that of Ambrose. The Eastern bishops at Chalcedon, which was most of them, could endure this humiliation only because Cyril's *Second Letter to Nestorius* and his *Letter to the Antiochenes* were incorporated into the faith statement. The ugly infighting that preceded Chalcedon in the twenty years after Ephesus—Alexandria still thought that Antioch had emerged with a measure of victory despite the condemnation of Nestorius—and that followed Chalcedon for the next 150 years, was over a basic question. Was Jesus truly one of us, a man of flesh and blood, or was his impassible and incorruptible human nature, rendered such by its union with the Word, in a class apart, hence not to be thought of as experiencing limit, passion, or temptation? Alexandria and Antioch were alike in their conviction that deity could not suffer, but the Cyrillians thought that Christ suffered only in his human nature, while the pupils of the Theodore of Mopsuestia (twenty-three years dead by the time of Chalcedon) thought that a man had suffered.

Hebrews had spoken of Jesus' dying with "loud cries and tears to God . . . learning obedience from what he suffered [and] made perfect [by it] . . . tempted in every way that we are, yet he never sinned" (5:7-9; 4:15). The hymn of 1 Timothy 2:5 was a stumbling block to Cyril because it spoke of "the man Jesus Christ" and "the one mediator between God and humanity" (see also Heb 8:6; 9:15; 12:24 for the designation "mediator"). The Alexandrians were largely unmoved by the testimony of the Gospels to Jesus as a limited and suffering human being. Their insistence on his single personhood, which had an ultimately impassible and immortal humanity as its chief effect, meant that this person could only be the Logos, using a human nature that could suffer as its instrument of salvation. They had their final triumph at II Constantinople in 553, whose *acta* the Roman bishop signed under pressure of Justinian, influenced by his now-dead, Monophysite-leaning wife Theodora. This council condemned as heretical portions of the writings of Theodore of Mopsuestia, Theodoret of Cyros and Ibas of Edessa. Basically, the authors of these "Three Chapters" had been marked by a stubborn insistence on the one person Jesus Christ as a human being intimately conjoined to the Logos, with all the limitations that humanness implies. Clearly, Cyril's "hypostatic" union of Jesus' humanity with the person of the Word, which Chalcedon had failed to teach, was to prevail a century later.

Chalcedon's genius resided in what it did not teach as much as in what it did. It was a compromise document that had reconciliation as its aim. This it did by proclaiming as the faith of the Church neither the theology of the indwelling Logos of the Antiochenes in its non-heretical form nor any notion of the hypostatic union that would jeopardize "the difference of the natures." It did teach a hypostatic union of sorts in declaring that the two natures were combined in "one person and hypostasis."[1] It clearly condemned the Eutychean extreme of the Cyrillian position by denying that the two natures were confused (*asygchýtōs;* he had confessed one single nature after the union[2]). But it omitted affirming that the birth, suffering, and death of Christ were real without thereby compromising the Godhead, which was the chief matter at issue. And it did not take a stand on whether "the activities and properties appropriate to each nature were to be appropriated ontologically only to that nature, even though verbally it might be permissible to predicate them of 'one and the same Christ.' "[3] The Catholic Church of East and West has lived with those unresolved questions ever since.

Second Constantinople tilted it toward the not quite Monophysite understanding that the Alexandrians had pressed for over the course of a century, all the while accusing Chalcedon of yielding to the Nestorian heresy. In the West the worship of "Jesus Christ as God" continued as part of the anti-Arian reaction going back to Nicea. But the medieval passion piety rooted in the teachings of the Cistercians and Saint Francis continued uninterrupted through the Reformation, chiefly through Luther and down to John Wesley and Alphonsus of Liguori. In the East the Russian piety of Christ the pilgrim sufferer was its match. This man, God though he was, endured pain, humiliation, and death, as one of us, to save us.

The Eucharistic texts promulgated at the direction of the Second Council of the Vatican share in all the settlements arrived at in the "Definition of the Faith" of 451—and all the ambivalence caused by its silences.

If W. S. Gilbert was right in saying "That every boy and every gal, / That's born into the world alive, / Is either a little Liberal, / Or else a little Conservative," then surely every Catholic Christian is born an Alexandrian or an Antiochene. This can result in ugly accusations that one's opponents do not believe in the divinity of Christ or that they do not take the New Testament seriously when it makes clear that he was human. Both sides in any such shouting match or curial charge can be faulted for not going back to their Chalcedonian roots to learn how much latitude is allowed, both by what is said and what is unsaid there. A clearly two-persons or one-nature heretic would be easy to identify, should one appear. Bilateral conversations between Catholic and pre-Chalcedonian Church theologians are disclosing how unlike the Nestorian and Monophysite heretics they are supposed to be, these theologians sound. Their positions are perilously close to, when not identical with, those of fifth-century Eastern Orthodox thought, largely unchanged over the ages. And when you hear Eastern congregations, Orthodox or Catholic, sing out strongly, "O, Our Christ God," forty or fifty times in one divine liturgy, you truly wonder if the "orthodoxy" of Chalcedon was ever absorbed.

What of the Christology of our parishes in the study, the very point at issue? The clearest indication given by the meager data is that it is a servant Christology—Jesus the washer of his servants' feet, whose disciples have done as he said they must do, following his example (see John 13:14-15). The Marcan Christology is, like the Johannine, a soteriology. There the Son of Man gives his life as a ransom for the many and in so doing is one who serves, not one who is served (Mark 10:45). Anything that can be deduced of how the people of these parishes view themselves indicates that as people "of Christ" (the phrase is uniquely Mark's, at the "cup of water" passage, 9:41), they are at the service of those who belong to him—and anyone else in need of their prayers and ministrations. It cannot be learned what effect the homilies are having. These are reported, without exception, as exhortations to do the work of justice in society. Certainly that was the teaching of Jesus as the condition for entering into God's rule, into the blessedness of his Father (Matt 25:34). The theme of mutual service is everywhere apparent in the study, not only in the exercises of ministries ordained and unordained but in the posture that all who are interviewed have toward each other. The universal respect and affection for pastor-presiders is a not insignificant clue to the christology they convey by word and deed. "There are occasions," Saint John Chrysostom says in a homily,

> on which there is no difference at all between the priest and the layperson, as, for example, when we are to partake of the awe-

some mysteries, for we are all alike counted worthy of the same things. Under the Old Covenant the priest ate some things, and those below him others, but it was not lawful for the people to partake of the things of which the priest partook. It is not that way now, but one body and one cup are set before all. . . . Note how frequently the apostles admitted the laity to share in their decisions. . . . No haughtiness of the rulers, not servility of the ruled.[4]

Chrysostom's spirit if not his letter is acted out by the numerous presiders whom the people admire for partaking of the Eucharistic meal last. (While this practice is taken as edifying in our table culture, there are those cultures where it could have the opposite effect.) The presiders' exhortations to stay to the end of Mass, and the evident disgust of the active parishioners with those who don't, can be found almost word for word in a series of sermons of Saint Caesarius of Arles (d. 542).[5] And Anastasius, Patriarch of Antioch (d. 608/09), speaks to some of the study's interviewees annoyed at those who do not seem to attend to the Canon before and after the words of consecration: "And when he is offering the bloodless Sacrifice, if he lingers even for a short time, we are bored and depressed, we yawn, and are as anxious to escape quickly from prayer as from a trial in court."[6]

The "lingering" spoken of could be in our day an expanded canon, the phrases of which have not been sufficiently committed to memory beforehand. They are more likely to be prefaces, canons, and prayers, each of which in the Roman Rite has a distinct Christology that can be missed if the rhetorical balance of the written piece is not caught by the spoken voice. Those parts of a spoken or sung liturgy are likely to make an impact if they are *heard*, and heard to speak in the lapidary fashion in which they are composed. Wasted words in the liturgy not only will not be heard; they are a threat to the words that do say something. I have never been in the chorus of those who moan at the ICEL translations, assuming they are decent human products that, like their Latin originals, can always be improved on. When their Christology is weak, as when they suggest that Jesus is like us in his humanness but not exactly one of us, or their Trinitarian theology deplorable, as in the preface and prayers of the feast of the Holy Trinity, I correct them orally as I shudder at what is written. I trust that all with firm theological sensibilities do the same.

How could one pass a true judgment on the Christologies that are transmitted and, it is hoped, received in any group of fifteen parishes? I have indicated what I have deduced. Christ as the Pauline head of a body-Church. Christ as the Johannine Son, not slave, who is heir in the household, setting others free. Christ as the Marcan servant, not a person served, who gives his life as a ransom-price, "complete in his deity and complete—the very same—in his humanity, truly God and truly a human being, this very same one being composed of a rational soul and a body, coessential with the Father as to his deity and coessential with us—the very same one—as to his humanity being like us in every respect apart from sin." That last is from the statement of faith of Chalcedon. If we have to make a creedal affirmation every Sunday, and I favor it, I wish it were this instead of Nicea–I Constantinople with its anti-Arian phrases that roll in on the ear like waves on the shore.

I named a few New Testament Christologies in the summary just above. There are more, many more than those elicited by heresy in the anathemas and creeds of the fourth and fifth centuries. Just as they came out of ancient political struggles, so modern Christologies are being forged by the sufferings of the dispossessed, the sense of alienation of Western Christian women. None of this is echoed in the study. How was Hebrews preached on, or not preached on, in the seven waning Sundays of the Mark year just behind us? How will the Christology of Revelation fare in the six Sundays after Easter of the Luke year we have just begun? As well as the opening passage from it in the Chrism Mass at the cathedral church? Better? Worse? And the Christology of the authentic letters of Paul, which we tend to get in six verses or less, often parenetic without their base in the mystery of Christ. I read everything that was said in the study about preaching, and I cannot guess at the answer.

The phrasing of the petitions, the interspersed comments of presiders, and the headings for readings, I feel more comfortable in my guesswork. That prose should be at ease in the way it speaks of all that God has done for us in Christ and all we must do for each other in the power of Holy Spirit. I say I feel secure here about its Christological spirit, informed by lack of reading and study of the Church's traditions, and if it is not drowned in words.

*Notes*

1. The analysis is from Jaroslav Pelikan, *The Christian Tradition*, vol. 1, *The Emergence of the Catholic Tradition (100–600)* (Chicago: University of Chicago Press, 1971) 263–269.

2. In the *Acta* of Chalcedon, 527. Strasbourg: *Acta Conciliorum Oecumenicorum*, 1914–. 2-I-I:143, cited by Pelikan, 262.

3. Pelikan, 265.

4. John Chrysostom, *Homily on Second Corinthians* 18.3, PG 61.527–528. Cited in Daniel Sheerin, *The Eucharist*, Message of the Fathers of the Church 7 (Wilmington: Michael Glazier, 1986). Translation revised by the author from that of the Library of Nicene and Post–Nicene Fathers. P. 324.

5. Caesarius of Arles, *Sermons* 73 and 74, ''Admonition to Stay to the End,'' Sheerin, *The Eucharist*, 326–332.

6. Anastasius II, Patriarch of Antioch, ''Sermon on the Eucharistic Assembly,'' PG 89.825–849, cited in Sheerin, *The Eucharist*, 338.

# Twenty-Five Years of a Wakening Church: Liturgy and Ecclesiology

*Monika K. Hellwig*

Being Church involves a great deal more than being in church for Sunday Eucharist and other forms of communal prayer. Yet there is no doubt that what happens at the Sunday Eucharist has more influence than any other factor on the way in which we envision the Church and our own role within it. That is why one can say immediately that the reports from the parishes in this survey are very encouraging; they do indeed show a trend toward assimilation of the ecclesiology of Vatican II.

Vatican II did, of course, initiate a shift in many aspects of our theology of the Church, but I have selected for comment six particular directions of change in the post–Vatican II Church and six points of emphasis in the ecclesiology of Vatican II that seem to correspond with the six types of change.[1] The directions of change that seem particularly important in relation to the way in which the Sunday Eucharist is celebrated are the following: the shift from a heavily clerical to an actively lay Church; the move from a rigidly centralized to a lively local Church; the opening out from a culturally European to a world Church; the blossoming from an almost exclusively ritual participation into a broad realization of the social and political implications of being a member of the Church; the consequent transformation from a rather quiescent to a diaconal membership, or at least the beginnings of such a transformation; and, finally, the dramatic awakening of a significant number of Catholics from seeing the Church as a maintenance function in society and history to seeing it as an essentially prophetic function.

55

It is my intention in this paper to describe these shifts as I see them in the Church at large, relating them specifically to the testimonies from the parishes in the study, and then to consider the emphases in the ecclesiology of Vatican II that seem to validate these shifts as authentic developments, suggesting some pastoral and liturgical implications for the future. Those emphases in the ecclesiology of Vatican II are the following: the organic-dynamic rather than static-institutional role of the Church in human history; collegiality as constitutive of Church; enculturation as perennial and necessary; the renewed awareness of prophetic vocation; the Church as essentially missionary, that is, as having a task not only for its own members but for the world; and a new realization of the worldly and temporal dimensions of healing and reconciliation in the calling of the Church to continue the mission of Christ in the world.

The most obvious shift in the way in which the Church exists and functions since the Second Vatican Council is the move from being a heavily clerical to an actively lay Church. By this, I mean that our pre–Vatican II Catholic Church was divided rather sharply into clergy as active members and laity as passive members, clergy as administering sacraments and preaching and laity as "receiving" sacraments and listening, clergy as conducting the essential work of the Church and laity as financing it. The shift away from this in the Church at large is clearly reflected in the parishes of this survey and is mirrored in interesting ways in the Sunday liturgies there described.

We become aware of ourselves as Church when we gather in a concrete event. In this survey, when Catholics gather for Sunday worship, there is in most cases a gathering place where parishioners greet one another and talk. That is a small point that seems to be very important because it establishes the understanding that Church has to do with relating to one another in a network of relationships and not only relating to God in prayer. Moreover, in many of the parishes of this survey there are people appointed to welcome the congregation as they arrive, and these seem generally to be volunteer laypeople from the parish. That is also important because the very nature of Church is outreach, community, overcoming of barriers and isolation, reconciliation among groups that have been mutually exclusive. That laypeople should be responsible for welcoming the congregation in general, and newcomers in particular, proclaims more clearly than any sermon could do that the people *are* the Church, called upon to do the work of the Church. In the past, Protestant Churches, especially in smaller sects and in smaller congregations, have been much better examples of this than Catholic communities; we seem at last to be rediscovering a missing dimension of the Church.

These first impressions seem to be well justified by what we learn in the survey about the planning and conduct of the Sunday liturgy—extensive teamwork of musicians, church decorators, planners of the celebration as a whole, lectors, extraordinary ministers of the Eucharist, and so forth. Therefore, the sense of belonging and of community that is built up in the course of the Sunday celebration must be informed by the subtle, subliminal if not explicit awareness of multiple patterns of initiative, activity, and relationship crisscrossing among the participants. And this in itself is surely helping to shift consciousness toward the ecclesiology of Vatican II, and therefore toward a richer ecclesiology recapturing elements that were lost or badly attenuated in recent centuries.

Although all the signs point in this direction, it would be fanciful to read the findings of the survey as though we had attained a wholly active, dynamic Church with a fully involved lay membership. The actual reports suggest in many cases that heroic efforts are being made by the noble few, and that there may be some danger that efforts to reform liturgical participation "from above" could lead not so much to a more involved congregation as to the formation of a kind of paraclergy, a self-selected small group of liturgical ministers, saving the congregation the trouble of active personal participation in ways analogous to those in which the pre–Vatican II rigidly defined and strictly clerical mode of celebration did. Perhaps this is a problem not susceptible of fuller solution in large congregations of Catholics who feel a strong sense of obligation to be present every Sunday, no matter what the other pressures in their lives may be.

Both the shift just described and the resistance to it seem to be connected with the second direction of change—from the heavily centralized Church of the pre–Vatican II era to the awakening initiatives of the local Churches. It is well known that this has been an area of extreme tension. The problematic lack of canonical status for episcopal conferences has left bishops in a situation of uncertainty and of vulnerability in the presence of self-appointed guardians of orthodoxy and orthopraxis. The all-too-evident difference of perspective and expectation between the postconciliar commission guidelines for implementation and the restraining hands of the established Vatican staff tends to introduce a note of discouragement even in the liveliest congregations.

Yet there is no doubt that the initiative of the local Church is getting an opportunity in the planning and conduct of liturgies, and in shared responsibility in RCIA (Rite of Christian Initiation of Adults) and other parish activities, which must change the impression that important Church decisions are always made centrally and handed down to the local Churches without adaptation. The change in awareness may be subtle and slow but must inevitably transform the pattern of relationships and the self-image of the local Churches.

Perhaps the most encouraging trend noticeable in the survey parishes is the tentative but discernible realization on their part of a vocation to be world Church and not culturally European in a dogmatically exclusive pattern. This is, of course, a challenge over which many generations before us puzzled and prayed, often coming to conclusions that in retrospect seem too timid.[2] But there are many indications in this survey that with extensive lay involvement there is more freedom for patterns of interaction and religious expression to emerge ''from below'' with a certain spontaneity, and cultural differences emerge between Hispanic, black, Acadian, and Asian groups, in addition to the long-accepted characteristic devotional and social patterns of Italian, Irish, and German local communities of Catholics in the United States.

This quiet and progressive pattern of enculturation seems to be a very important aspect of a Church becoming more authentically and pervasively redemptive. It probably also offers a better basis for American Catholics to see themselves as members of a world Church in which the problems and questions that preoccupy the more literate and vocal among mainstream North American Catholics may not be the most urgent or practical for the Church in other populations and cultures. There are certainly signs that the Catholic Church of the United States is becoming less alien and superimposed for minorities, and that the majority is becoming more aware of the cultural variety that the Church can and must encompass.

These converging trends have also meant that the Church in general has been making a post–Vatican II shift from exclusively ritual and private moral considerations toward a more political understanding of the redemptive and ecclesial task. This is perhaps the change in outlook that is coming most slowly and with the most resistance from many Catholics. A rather extensive rethinking of the faith and of the Christian commitment is involved in the realization that redemption in Christ and the restoration of the reign of God in the world encompasses all dimensions of human life and activity—all the relationships, values, expectations, societal structures, and systems. Such realization threatens existing privilege and calls for all kinds of disruption of accustomed patterns and routines, demanding extra effort, time, and attention.

The parishes in the survey seem to show both involvement in public and social issues and a certain hesitation or reluctance in such matters. While all report some social action committees or groups and some concern with issues of social justice and peace, it would seem that most see such concern as important but nevertheless peripheral to the real task of a parish. It may be because this was really a liturgical survey that the responses were necessarily focused so that liturgy would occupy the center of the stage and would appear as self-sustaining and self-justifying. In any case, the liturgy in these reports is less like the peak or summit of a very full and active Christian life in the world and looks more like the whole landscape.

Nevertheless, the move from a rather acquiescent sense of Church to one more directly and explicitly diaconal is evident in the multiplicity of parish activities and of groups designated to take care of these activities. Perhaps the strong community base and natural sense of solidarity inclines minority Churches and Churches with a strong minority component more spontaneously toward multiple practical ministries responding to the actual day-to-day needs of the community and its members. Affluent parishes in an urban setting, with mainstream Caucasian membership, seem to be more attuned to "buying" help from the available secular services of the area. But it is evident from this survey that the structuring of community upon an outreach to meet the needs of others has increasingly become an element in the sense of what a parish should be.

It is true that charitable and neighborly concern and practical help has always been proposed as a Christian duty, but it is not clear that in the pre–Vatican II Church such charitable concern was generally seen as being of the very essence of the Church's task in history. Nor is it clear that any actual change in conditions of life was really expected in the Christian community, in spite of familiarity with the pictures of Christian community painted in the Acts of the Apostles. For most Catholics it would seem that such expectations would have been associated with the ecclesiology of the Anabaptist Churches and not with the Catholic ecclesiology that they themselves professed. What seems to be emerging as an outcome of Vatican II is a clearer sense that being Church means a transformation of all attitudes and relationships and therefore involves an attitude of ministry in all aspects of life and relationships.

Finally, all of this leads to a shift from Church seen as essentially a maintenance operation to Church seen as prophetic. In the U.S. Church this has been very evident in the stances taken by the Bishops' Conference on abortion, race, poverty, and nuclear armaments. But much of this thrust does not seem to be coming from the grass roots of the Church communities. In the reports and discussions of this survey it seemed to me that the prophetic character of the Church was least emphasized. As mentioned before, that may be partly due to the fact that it was intended to be a study of parish liturgies rather than primarily a study of their ecclesiology or of their outward activities. Yet one has the sense that for most of the people in these parishes, the Church is still more a maintenance function than a revolutionary force in the world to restore the reign of God in all those aspects and dimensions of society in which it is the personal, partisan, or national quest for power or wealth or status that reigns over human affairs and societal decisions.

However, taken as a whole the testimonies in these reports are impressive and indicate a Church in process of waking up and assuming responsibility for its mission. We must assume, I think, that the parishes that agreed to be part of this survey and study are exemplary rather than typical, but the news that reaches us from them is encouraging. It shows what can be done in U.S. parishes of all types, and it shows what a splendid beginning has been made in some parishes, which can then serve as models for others.

These developments correspond very well to the ecclesiology proposed or implied by the Second Vatican Council. As is well known and as has already been much discussed in publications,[3] Vatican II moved far beyond the then almost exclusively institutional way of thinking about the nature and function of the Church to retrieve and incorporate into our ecclesiology the many images and analogies of Scripture and tradition: the flock, the people of God, the pilgrim people, the vineyard, the followers of the Way, and many more. *Lumen gentium* (the Dogmatic Constitution on the Church) opens with the idea of a people assembling and being reconstituted as the people of God, using this dynamic and clearly personal and interpersonal model of the Church as the basic one for further reflection on what the whole community of believers should be and do. And this more vital conception of Church is further developed in its practical implications in the other documents of the council. Most especially it is developed in *Sacrosanctum concilium* (The Constitution on the Sacred Liturgy), which envisages the laity as actively involved and as transforming their lives and societies by the light of a new vision of human possibilities constantly unfolded in their liturgical participation. But also in *Gaudium et spes* (the Pastoral Constitution on the Church in the Modern World) the council developed a more vital understanding of Church in its explorations of the political and prophetic dimensions essential to both local and universal Church.

This essay will not repeat the analysis of the models of Church involved, because that has been done many times and is easily accessible. Indeed, some of the interviews in the parish study have already considered the models of Church that might best fit the activities and patterns of interaction described in particular parish communities of the survey. This essay will take a different approach in considering some changes in our ecclesiology that appear to be mandated by Vatican II.

The first of these is the retrieval of an organic-dynamic rather than institutional-static expectation of the role that the Church must play in history. The recapturing of a biblical and patristic sense of Church has meant a return to the understanding that the Church does not exist for its own sake but for the sake of the coming reign of God in the whole human community and in all creation. That is why it is aptly described as a pilgrim people, a people on the march, moving toward a goal that has not yet been reached and structuring its activities and relationships in whatever way is most apt to help reach the goal. This is a future-oriented way of thinking about Church and what the community of disciples should be doing in changing circumstances and contexts, contrasted with a way of thinking that is based upon the past as having established an adequate structure and content for an unchanging perennial presence in the world and its history. Vatican II shows clearly the conviction that in the course of history the world changes, societies and their experiences change, people's needs and opportunities change, and therefore the tasks for the Church change and the communities of believers must adapt to find the contemporary forms of fidelity to the mission of welcoming the reign of God into human society.

This renewed understanding that the Church is a people on the move is connected with a second change in our ecclesiology in and after Vatican II. That is the recovery of a more vital and existential sense of mission. Again, this is a return to sources, a recovery of the original impetus, a renewal rather than an innovation. There seems to have been a certain reductionism in Church life and attitudes in recent centuries and especially since the Enlightenment. The sense of Church was commonly reduced to the obligation and privilege of churchgoing and conformity to some special rules for private life. We measured a good Catholic as one who attended Mass every Sunday without fail, remained faithful to the sacraments, kept all explicit rules, married within the Catholic community, and sent the children to Catholic schools. The problem that manifests itself in this set of expectations is not only the passivity of the individuals within the structure but also the effective isolation of the faithful Catholic community from contemporary culture and from the shaping of society's values and activities.

What has happened in the documents of Vatican II is a critical rethinking of the dimension of mission—as it relates to the community of the faithful in their own lives and interaction and as it relates to the impact that Catholics can and should have on the society at large. The sense that there is a task to do and that this task belongs to all the baptized is very important in its consequences. It suggests that critical intelligence must be at work in the living of a Christian life. But it also suggests that there must be resources, criteria, by which ordinary believers can constantly be appraising the situations in which they live and work in order to judge them by the light of the gospel and act accordingly. Hence, the enormously increased importance of the liturgical Scripture readings and the homilies, which should bring them into play with contemporary life. While we thought of the role of the Catholic laity mainly in terms of churchgoing and the obeying of explicit commands and rules, the Scripture readings in the liturgy could be mainly for inspiration and encouragement and consolation in a general way. Once we begin, however, to take the mission of the Church seriously as the vocation of all the baptized, the Scriptures become the continuing formation of the Christian conscience in a vital and critical way.

Moreover, it is not only in the hearing of and reflecting on the Scriptures that the community needs to find the vision and the criteria for judging and acting in the contemporary world. The liturgy as such is clearly intended to shape human perception of the world, human society, and its history and possibilities. The participation in the liturgy as a whole is supposed to be creating the vision of what the Church might be and how the Church, that is, the community of disciples, might be reshaping their own smaller social circle and through it the larger society. For instance, the kiss of peace is not supposed to be selectively directed to one's chosen friends but to all those who happen to be around. Likewise, the active participation in the liturgical celebration is supposed to be not the special task and privilege of a small elite but distributed as widely as possible through the congregation. Communion received in the hand is a more adult and responsible gesture than the former tradition of Communion laid on the tongue. Community preparation of church building, music, and details of the ritual suggests Church as something we are all doing together rather than a ready-made institution that functions on our behalf.

Taken one by one, these are all rather small points and may often seem more trouble than they are worth. Yet cumulatively they are creating in the imagination a certain image of the Church and a certain expectation of what it means to be a member of the Church. And cumulatively such experiences are therefore of great importance for the way in which this and future generations of Catholics will understand their role. The more actively and widely the congregation is involved in the liturgy, the more likely individual Catholics are to see the Church as essentially a mission in the world—a mission to transform and to welcome the reign of God with its harmony and its justice—and the more likely they are to see themselves as called to active participation in that mission.

That more vital sense of mission, in turn, connects with the Vatican II emphasis on collegiality. It is true that the documents of Vatican II refer explicitly only to the collegiality of the bishops and of the clergy within a diocese. Yet it is evident that the principle, once established, rediscovers the whole nature of the Church at all levels. The Church cooperates with the risen Christ in the completion of the work of redemption. That means it is the task of the Church to cooperate in the welcoming of the reign of God, which is always at hand within us and among us. All that is lacking is human recognition of it, and the reordering of our lives accordingly. What this means is the reversing of the disorders of sin in the world. But the chief disorder of sin is the assertion of the self as the center, leading to the rejection of God and of the claims of others. This results in our world in extensively elaborated and sanctioned bullying patterns. It is not the strong dictatorial structures of human society that best reflect God's order in creation but the cooperative, collaborative patterns that acknowledge the creativity and intelligence of all concerned. It is not class distinctions and pyramids of special status that reflect best what Jesus taught his disciples according to the Gospels or what they understood according to the Acts of the Apostles. Far rather, it is the overcoming of all these that is indicated in the New Testament as the work of the kingdom and the manifestation of the grace of Christ in a community.

Hence, the principle of collegiality is not simply a concession to the modern age or a compromise to appease a more democratically educated community. The commitment to work by consensus and involve all who are willing to cooperate is at the very heart of the Church's task in the redemption, because it is the commitment to reverse the false relationships of sin and the bullying patterns they involve. This is an implication of Vatican II that has been only very reluctantly accepted if at all, both in the central Roman administration of the institutional Church and, often, in the local Churches. Our reaction to the Protestant Reformers of the sixteenth century was to emphasize the special roles of clergy and hierarchy even more than before because they had been challenged by the Reformers, and to emphasize the central control of the universal Church heavily at the expense of local initiative and vitality for the same reason. Vatican II began to correct the focus and that process is still slowly evolving. The very shape of the liturgical celebration at the parish level should be stimulating and supporting the imagination and expectation of the parish community to see Church in those terms.

A further change in our ecclesiology that came about at and after Vatican II is the affirmation of the principle of enculturation. This refers to the mode of relationship that the Church with its ancient tradition should adopt toward societies whose cultures are widely different from the European heritage in which the Church is historically rooted. There is, of course, both in the universal Church, and in particular situations such as the parishes of this survey, a tension between the need for unity and the need for authentic enculturation in the particular lives of minority or recently incorporated groups. The Church has felt that tension throughout its history and has struggled with efforts to accommodate both kinds of needs. The post–Vatican II Church in the world has by no means resolved the tensions in practice, but the principle has been explicitly acknowledged: The Church must not be alien in culture to any of its members; it should be something that they can own as their expression and activity; it should enable them to act upon their own culture, not to change it to an alien one but to draw out of its own resources the best ways of achieving justice, peace, dignity, and community for all.

In the light of this, there seems to be room for further reflection on whether the needs of minority groups in the parishes of the survey are being fully met. Such reflection must, of course, take many factors into account. We are not dealing with communities of other cultures in their home setting but as immigrants to this country. In many cases they may be very anxious to adapt and be assimilated, using English as much as possible and mixing with the English-speaking congregation. Yet we know that there are many refugees among us who were forced to flee their country but hope to return and want to keep their own cultural heritage intact. Moreover, there has been a certain rethinking and hesitation over the movement of racial integration in this country. Black communities have begun to wonder whether they may be losing elements of their traditional lives that were not simply examples of cultural deprivation but of cultural richness and particularity. It is clear that at least one parish in this survey is meeting that concern with enthusiasm and appropriate sensitivity. Nevertheless, it does seem surprising that there is not more indication in the other parishes of the survey of Sunday Eucharists, festivals, baptisms, and the like in the style adapted to particular minority groups, especially that of the black and Hispanic communities. There may be more being done in that line than appears in the survey, but the matter seems to be worth further discussion and reflection.

Not unconnected with this issue of enculturation is the renewed sense in Vatican II that *diakonia*, service of human needs, is an essential aspect of the mission of the Church. The ministries recorded in the Acts of the Apostles were astonishingly varied: the visiting of the sick and housebound, provision for widows and orphans and others who were poor, and so forth. In the course of the centuries, the Christian countries gradually assumed many of these tasks into the responsibilities of the secular society, exercised through its government and administration. Moreover, modern technology has both extended our knowledge and responsibility and changed it to far more complex and technically specialized tasks. It is not surprising, then, that the sense of these practical services, as routinely part of the life of a Christian community, has diminished a good deal over the course of time and needed to be brought to the fore again. The notion of ministry has come to be associated with those functions that required an ordination or at least a special designation in the name of the Church. That means, of course, that the term has tended to be restricted to liturgical and preaching activites. The whole tenor of the documents of Vatican II and of the actions the institutional Church has taken upon those documents has suggested a far wider understanding of what the essential ministries of the Church are. On the whole, this seems to be reflected by the practice at least of the parishes in the survey. It may take longer to achieve an acknowledgment of this wider understanding in the ecclesiology and sacramental theology that are accepted and explicitly acknowledged in those parishes. In the parishes of the survey, just as in the current practice of theology and catechesis of the Church at large, there still seems to be the sense that liturgical worship is the real business of the Church and that healing, reconciliation, and the service of practical human needs in all their forms are optional additions for those with that particular charism or inclination. It may be worthwhile to discuss and consider further whether, through the liturgy itself, more may be done to suggest a more comprehensive sense of what constitutes the ministries of the Church.

The last of the characteristics of post–Vatican II ecclesiology to be considered here is the shift to a more concretely and immediately prophetic stance in relation to the large issues of social justice and peace in our contemporary society. This point was evident in the documents of Vatican II themselves, has been emphasized in subsequent papal encyclical letters since, and has been especially pronounced in the utterances of some of the episcopal conferences including our own in the United States. The statements made by the U.S. Bishops' Conference after broad consultation in the Catholic community and in the wider society—statements about racial and economic justice and about peacemaking and the need to reverse the armaments race—have been a strong thrust in the direction of a prophetic Church. In spite of the wide consultation, however, it is not evident that the Catholic laity is generally in support of the more critical stances taken in the bishops' letter. The testimony from the parishes in this survey suggests that in the planning of parish activities, including liturgical worship, there are careful efforts made to present a prophetic presence and action in the world as an essential element of the living of the Christian life and of the building of a Christian community. Yet this is probably the area of ecclesiology that requires the most tactful but persistent challenge to existing values and assumptions.

The history of the Catholic Church as a whole in the modern world, and the history of the United States Catholic Church in particular, have not prepared most Catholics for the understanding that their faith and Church membership may pit them against prevailing national and cultural values. We have recognized some specific instances of this countercultural stance in such issues as pornography and abortion, but we have expected to find ourselves in step with prevailing ideas in areas such as national security, liberal capitalism, accepted tax structures, and so forth. The suggestion that we may be called upon to question or oppose the respectable values of the society or to take issue with political platforms that are in our own economic interest is coming as a rather rude awakening to Catholics in this country. We have been used to the assumption that such stances belong to the ecclesiology of the Society of Friends and the Mennonites and other such Christian communions but that the Catholic Church sees its relationship to our own government and national interest as one of almost unqualified support and endorsement. That it might be otherwise is not easy to assimilate and therefore suggests a particularly careful reflection and strategy in the guidance of parish activities and in the focus of attention in parish liturgies.

## Conclusion

In summary, it may be said that the implicit ecclesiology of the reports included in the survey is most assuredly that of the Second Vatican Council and of the implications that have unfolded from it. But it may also be said that much of the content of those implications is yet to be assimilated, and that we may expect that process to take time. To say that we may expect it to take time, however, is not to say that the assimilation of a more vital, collegial, active, and prophetic ecclesiology may be expected to come about without deliberate effort. The continued valiant work of parish leadership by dedicated, reflective, and challenging people is much needed.

## Notes

1. The documents of Vatican II directly concerned are the Dogmatic Constitution on the Church, the Pastoral Constitution on the Church in the Modern World, and The Constitution on the Sacred Liturgy. However, all the documents of the council as well as subsequent official instructions and guidelines for implementation have a bearing on the topic under discussion.

2. Examples are the imposition of foreign names, clothes, and customs on the Indian Christians of Goa; the failure to recognize the more spontaneous styles of

religious expression in African, Caribbean, and U.S. black communities; the difficulties over Chinese ancestral and civic rites, and so forth.

3. The seminal work is that of Avery Dulles, *Models of the Church* (New York: Doubleday, 1974), suggesting five basic models: institution, mystical communion, sacrament, herald, and servant, to which Father Dulles later added the more generic model: community of disciples.

# Symbol in Liturgy, Liturgy as Symbol: The Domestication of Liturgical Experience

*Don E. Saliers*

At the 1974 gathering of the North American Academy of Liturgy at Notre Dame I recall reporting to the plenary from one of the discussion groups a proposal that we should undertake a detailed inquiry of case studies of liturgical celebrations drawn from actual parish life. We had already begun to discern the need for something more than comparative textual inquiry. We wanted detailed access to the phenomena of the rites enacted by actual assemblies in specific cultural settings. It is therefore a delight and a responsibility to have been asked to contribute to our common assessment of the conciliar reforms in light of this study, so teeming with data from living, if not lively, parishes. While these studies do not achieve a full ethnographic description and show a noticeable lack of reference to the conciliar documents and guidelines, they do provide a provocative mix of evaluative and descriptive modes of presentation. Or, one might say, this survey serves up the raw and the cooked together.

While my assignment is to comment from the standpoint of symbolic theory, I must warn you at the outset that the matter of symbol and symbolic efficacy in the liturgy cannot be discussed abstractly in light of the survey. The pastoral and theological issues it raises in my reading are deeply intertwined with questions concerning the symbolic nature of liturgy. And since this survey is positively toxic with affectivity, issues concerning relations between symbolic perception, human emotion, and religious experience will be given special attention. It will become clear, I trust, that symbol and human emotion in liturgy are theological concerns and not simply a matter of the psychology of religious experience.

But I also come as one who knows firsthand the problems of liturgical reform in Protestant Pietist traditions, often in places where American patterns of religious experience have domesticated the gospel. So you may also hear notes of warning and danger, born of pastoral-liturgical engagement in traditions struggling to recover symbol and ritual action in the midst of an undifferentiated sea of local piety. There are perennial tensions between formalism and enthusiasm, between fossilization and loss of symbolic range, between "back to Trent" and forward into American parochialism, that surface here. We need all the ecumenical insight we can get in order to allow the conciliar reforms to yet shape the emergent *reformanda* of Roman Catholic liturgy in North America.

### Primary Symbol and Liturgical Experience: Some Reminders

"Only if we come to the liturgy without hopes or fears, without longings or hunger, will the rites symbolize nothing and remain indifferent or curious 'objects.' Moreover, people who are not accustomed to poetic, artistic or musical language or symbolic acts among their means of expression and communication find the liturgy like a foreign country whose customs and language are strange to them."[1]

Thus, Joseph Gelineau, writing a decade ago in his insightful little volume, *The Liturgy Today and Tomorrow,* introduces one of our principal themes: The liturgy is itself a country we must learn to dwell in. It contains many languages and customs that form a crucible of experience, a multiple-layered culture. In our present stage of liturgical reform and renewal, now some quarter-century away from the initial sound of the trumpet, we sense with greater urgency than before the centrality of the double question of symbol in the liturgy and liturgy as symbol. We have learned to speak of the assembly gathered about the book, the font, and the table, and certainly we have come to see that liturgical research must develop increasing depth and sensitivity in attending to the concrete problems of ritual participation by specific communities. We know, in theory at least, that enacted liturgy, while trafficking in texts, is much more than texts well translated and ordered along with their accompanying rubrics (even elastic rubrics no longer in red). Enter the double question: symbol in liturgy and liturgy as symbol.

"Full, active, conscious participation" is only a receding slogan from The Constitution on the Sacred Liturgy if we do not attend to specific questions concerning resistance and vulnerability to the non-verbal and symbolic dimensions of liturgical celebration in specific social-cultural contexts. In our haste to render the liturgy intelligible and accessible to the worshipers, we easily neglect the complex matter of participation in symbol and symbolic efficacy (power and range). In our preoccupation with reformed texts and rubrics, we may have neglected the most difficult challenge: to uncover the intersection of human hopes and fears, longing and hungers, with the symbolic power and range of liturgical rites authentically celebrated. Put another way, the current situation, so tellingly reflected in the data of the survey, pushes us to reassess how we have conceived and fostered liturgical participation. We must think again about the second half of that famous sentence from paragraph 14 of The Constitution on the Sacred Liturgy: The Church "earnestly desires that all the faithful should be led to that full, conscious, and active participation in liturgical celebrations which is demanded by the very nature of the liturgy."

What about the "very nature of the liturgy," which calls forth and engenders certain modes of participation? For our purposes symbol is the heart of the matter—more specifically, what the symbols in the whole complex of the enacted rites demand of worshipers is the heart of the matter. It is the otherness of symbol and the demand of the liturgy itself as symbolic common action that I miss most in the gestalt of the data in the survey. The overwhelming impression is that these communities have focused on the "expressive" dimensions of participation rather than the inner relations between the formative and expressive power of primary symbol. Until the otherness of liturgical symbols is perceived and respected, it will be difficult to avoid rendering "participation" with any depth. That worshipers in these fifteen parishes have become more active is quite evident. What is less evident is how the modes of participation are related to the primary mystery of encounter with God's self-giving in word and sacramental sign-actions.

In reading the data it is clear that in nearly every parish situation, there are not only different levels of participation in symbolic action but a wide variety of conceptions of symbol. From awareness of eating and drinking as symbol to gestures with the book, joining hands for the Our Father (remarkably widespread) to the use of different colored carnations for catechumens and sponsors (referred to as a "nice symbol")—all seem to count. This can, of course, be regarded as a semantic matter; but it suggests a deeper problem of a failure to distinguish primary symbol from secondary, or worse, from expressive ornamentation. How are we to take the addition of the ritual act of naming children who are to have birthdays or the extra ceremonial with the Advent wreath? Are these pastorally sensitive moments of "participation" or, rather, accretions that seem to obscure the centrality of primary symbol? Let these questions hover for a while; an a priori answer is not appropriate. Only when we examine the whole context of ritual participation and the correlate modes of consciousness can an adequate assessment be made. But if in such liturgies there is minimal attentiveness to the Eucharistic Prayer or no evidence of contemplative interiorization of the readings or the homily, then answers to these questions begin to emerge.

There is, among all of these parishes, a concerted attention by the liturgy team and most of those interviewed to do the liturgy well. Again and again we learn of appreciation for the hospitality, the friendliness, the good sense of musical choice, and the smooth choreography of the liturgy. None of these values are, in themselves, detrimental to "good liturgy." But generally one looks in vain for references to the sense of transcendent mystery in the experience of primary symbols. The very conception of liturgical prayer and common prayerful participation is at stake here. As one group interview participant observes with respect to the responses, "To have it be really prayer" requires formation. The respondent goes on to say, "I'd like to see reeducation of everybody over thirty." (As though everyone under thirty were well formed!) The point is well taken, however: participation in symbolic action and entering into the demand and the otherness of the primary symbols does take "formation," formation at several levels. Catechesis and mystagogy still yearn to embrace in most of these parishes. Later, this point will be linked with the matter of levels of capacity for deep affections such as awe, gratitude, holy fear, repentance, joy in the midst of suffering, and hope. For now we turn to some reminders concerning the primary symbols in the context of liturgical participation.

### *"Otherness" of Ritual Symbol and Levels of Participation*

Mary Collins addresses the effort in contemporary liturgical studies to attend to "actual local practice, the customary usage of particular churches." In a chapter on ritual symbols and process she reminds us that the conciliar reforms generated a situation, especially in the

American Churches, that has thrown worshipers back on their own resources. She observes:

> They have worked with greater or lesser knowledge of the wider liturgical tradition and the official liturgy, past and pending. They have drawn on the depth or superficiality of their experience and understanding of the paschal mystery, the mystery of dying and rising which is celebrated in every liturgy. They have been more or less successful in distinguishing the truly archaic ritual symbols of the Christian liturgical tradition still capable of embodying faith, from the merely antiquated ritual forms of other eras. . . . Sometimes local worshipers have created ritual forms of sufficient vitality that they warrant inclusion in the public repertoire of the Roman Catholic Church. At other times, the banality of the forms or their esoteric qualities invite conscious repudiation and even banishment from the ritual repertoire.[2]

The failure to distinguish the primary or truly archaic symbols from ritual forms that express the inclinations of the present cultural modes of communication of the worshipers is a major problem across ecumenical lines. But it is a special problem for the Roman tradition so recently struggling to come out from under imprisoned and fossilized symbolization. Victor Turner's account of the three fundamental characteristics of ritual symbols may assist us in our discernment of where these parishes are with respect to the "double question" posed earlier, now amplified: How can our participation in symbol be true to the nature of Christian liturgy, and how can our experience of the liturgy be truly symbolic of the mystery that Christian liturgy signifies?

In his *Forest of Symbols* and "Forms of Symbolic Action: Introduction,"[3] Turner proposes that ritual symbols (1) possess multivocality, or a fusion of many levels of meaning, (2) have the power to unify several disparate referents and experiences, and (3) accumulate meanings around both affective and morally normative values. All three of these characteristic features of symbol work together in a live ritual context. It is of the very nature of liturgy that the central signs such as bread, wine, water, oil, along with communal actions such as eating and drinking, washing, laying on of hands, articulate and give expression to a particular range of meanings in the concrete situation of their being enacted by a community. Each liturgical celebration forms and expresses a selected range of the many levels of meaning inherent in the symbol and brings together in a unified experience both the sensate human dimensions of the symbol and the mystery signified by the biblical word of the divine-human interaction. It is over time that the fullness of symbol may be comprehended, if comprehended at all, by the worshiping assembly. The biblical word and the range of sacramental sign-actions provide a shared matrix of social meaning. With respect to Christian liturgy, the three interactive dimensions of symbol described by Turner depend in part on the discipline and the formed aesthetic imagination shared by the assembly. But this very discipline and imaginative capability must be congruent with the deepest range of meanings presented nondiscursively by the symbols activated in the ritual context. This is crucial to preserving the "otherness" of primary Christian symbols.

On the one hand, symbols can be spoken of as objects, gestures, utterances, complex actions. On the other hand, ritual symbols are never merely things. This is because "things" like light, water, oil, or bread are already, for the Christian tradition, embedded in a history of shared social life. Such objects are not themselves "symbolic" by virtue of using them to express our experience. Rather, only by being vulnerable to and learning to participate in the shared life toward which these symbols point is "experience of the symbol" possible. The paradox of ritual symbol is that in order for us to participate, the whole human being must be engaged through the senses (visible, acoustic, kinetic, and the like), while at the same time acknowledging that liturgical action signifies realities beyond immediate experience. Understanding ourselves to be in relation to divine reality is itself a parabolic, metaphoric, and symbolic process, as Turner's three points suggest.

Gelineau has put this point well:

> Ritual activity is not concerned with producing purely "worldly" effects . . . but the coming of the Kingdom. Thus in the liturgy we do not eat only to feed our bodies; we do not sing only to make music; we do not speak only to teach and to learn; we do not pray only to restore our psychic equilibrium. The liturgy is a parabolic type of activity (which throws us aside), metaphorical (which takes us somewhere else), allegorical (which speaks of something else) and symbolic (which brings together and makes connections).[4]

This excursus into ritual symbol implies that submitting to the otherness of symbol cannot be a simple, naive operation. It requires a deeper entry into the biblical word, which provides language, albeit inadequate and culturally embedded and particular (therefore requiring critical distance), descriptive and ascriptive of those mysteries into which we are invited and taken by the power of common ritual action.

Even the word—read, spoken, sung, contemplated—therefore becomes symbol. Unless, of course, we confine the word to its discursive or merely propositional level—reducing our preaching or hearing to listening for moral maxims and/or dogmatic truths, literally dispensed. (This is the great flaw of all fundamentalisms—biblical or ecclesial.) Perhaps one of the reasons for my impression of a certain one-dimensionality of symbol in the interviewees' responses is that relatively little connection is made therein with biblical catechesis (in comparison, say, with favorable or unfavorable responses to the content of the homily or the ''experience'' of the reading). When the referents and the narratives of Scripture are not available to the worshiping assembly, there is a diminishment of symbol. As Turner, Langer, Geertz, and other symbol theorists remind us, it is the multivocality and the unification of different referents and levels of experience—affective, cognitive, and moral-volitional—that constitutes the power of ritual symbols for human lives. In the world of biblical minimalism the typological and ''connecting'' power of the liturgy is reduced to connections in the human range of experience we bring. Biblical minimalism increases subjective projection onto the symbol (and, ironically, into the biblical texts themselves). The deeper power of ritual symbolism in the Easter Vigil or in the rites of reconciliation, for example, presupposes the ''archeology'' (Ricoeur) or the otherness of the story and the reality beyond our experience. The liturgy is not a static system or structure to which we bring our life experience; rather it is a crucible of meanings that, if entered with our whole humanity, makes experience possible: deeper gratitude, deeper awe, a greater capacity for suffering, hope, and compassion. Such emotional dispositions are not simply our cultural values found ''in'' the liturgy, but are in large measure patterned because of a special memory and a history not immediately ours.

Having said this, we must then stress the fact that liturgical participation itself is symbolic and parabolic. That is, participation in the ''sensible signs''—gathering, greeting, singing, listening, speaking, embracing, eating, drinking, blessing, being blessed—is only the first level of participation. At the second level we discern that enacting the liturgy together is participation in the mystery of being Church. This is precisely why ''doing the liturgy well'' is not enough. We can, as Protestant Evangelicalism should have taught us long since, worship in a lively, dramatic, and humanly engaging manner and yet not conceive our assembly as participating in the mystery of God's self-giving to the Church. Without this second level of participation, the liturgy itself will not symbolize. Here and there in the survey this awareness comes through clearly as in one pastor's remark: "It's like you dream . . . a vision . . . that people gather for prayer, worshiping, offering praise, thanksgiving, the music, the responding, singing. At some point they say, 'we could stay here forever.' That's the kingdom. . . ." Such awareness of the liturgy as symbol of the mystery of the Church and the rule and reign of God is more than "doing the liturgy smoothly" or "making it work." Yet, such a sense of participation in liturgy as symbol requires careful attention to the forms, the choreography, the space, the concrete actions of reading, singing, praying, movement, and the like.

Perhaps this point could be summarized by observing in classical fashion that there are three interrelated levels of participation in ritual symbol in the context of Christian liturgy. First is the necessary attentive participation at the level of the rites. Second, participation in the rites, fully, consciously, actively, must itself be discerned as an act of the Church—of the people of God called by word and sacrament to become in the world who we are in God's sight. Third, participation in liturgical rites and symbolic range is itself a participation in the rule and reign of God (the kingdom) already come and yet to come in fullness.

Now we are in a better position to turn to the question of how liturgy both shapes and expresses a community in affective life—in a patterning of emotions if you will. The awakening and sustaining of social capacity to respond to symbols is central. Perhaps the greatest task ahead of us in light of the data from this survey is to restore a sense of history and *mysterion* to the symbols embedded in the ritual actions of the liturgy. This process is both catechetical and mystagogical. It must always be evocative, imaginative, and experiential—but constantly grounded in the biblical witness to a living tradition. We never have access to the unmediated "pure" meaning of symbols. The water, the bread and wine, the cross, the word, always reveal and conceal. This requires bringing our cultural experience and pattern of life into contact with the otherness of the symbol-embedded word, and the word-permeated sign-action.

## Forming and Expressing the Affective Dimensions of Liturgy

We observed earlier that ritual symbol orients us to both the affective and the morally normative dimensions of human existence. Much is made in the survey of the expressive and experiential dimensions of liturgical celebrations. In most of the parishes we sense an earnest search for "moving" liturgical experience. More than once we overhear persons speaking of "being touched" by some gesture, by a procession, or by serving others at Eucharist. Now, for a tradition climbing out from under an overly clericalized and hierarchically controlled sense of objective rites with little attention to the *operantis* or subjective dispositions of the worshipers, such a search for "experienced immediacy" within the rites is understandable. But this is precisely the principal problem these pietistically sensitized ears and eyes of mine discern. A short excursus is in order.

We soon discover that what we can "experience" of a particular event in our lives in the immediacy of its engagement—even (and perhaps most especially) when we are fully participating—is but a selective range of the whole set of meanings that event reveals after time. Even the notion of immediacy of "feeling" deals principally with what is selected out of the rich and largely inchoate and often concealed pattern that is present to our consciousness. Consider, for example, our experience of other persons at a family reunion. We hear Uncle Fred tell the old stories, we may indeed meet a new cousin or engage another relative at a new level of discourse, we may eat the foods (often placed on the table in a highly ordered sequence—with Grandma Mytrie's creamed fruit salad last because it has become a ritual dessert) and yet only receive part of the significance of the persons and the gathering. We go through a complex array of meeting, talking, eating, singing, and telling common stories but only catch certain elements and aspects of what is present in the event. We come away, as do many of the parishioners in our survey, with a kind of general feel of the whole liturgy, with an impressionistic sense of the whole, punctuated here and there with vivid moments of recollection.

My point is simply this: We should be cautious about assigning too much valence to the experienced "immediacies of feeling." Even when asked, "What was most meaningful, or what were you feeling during the Communion rite?" we can only speak from a first level of awareness. What is revealed in the responses in reporting immediacy of feeling-response are precisely powerful currents of human consciousness, which are triggered by particular features of the liturgical action and the symbols. This is seen in one example from Holy Redeemer Parish in the person who came to the liturgy aware of her father's illness. At several points this person drifted into the sense of "a lot of pain" in the world. She became very involved in the singing of the *Gloria*, and at various points in the liturgy. Then she observed, "But . . . again I think I was thinking about my dad." Later, during the Eucharistic Prayer in the post-*Sanctus*, she remarked, "I remember thinking about my husband's grandmother who passed away. And an aunt of mine. . . ." These are vivid reports of consciousness triggered by participation. What we do not see is how, over time, liturgical participation may have given and/or deepened her capacity to make the connections.

Thus, immediacy of feeling must be distinguished from depth of emotion. It is the "depth of emotion" that only shows up over time. Only when connections such as the above are made in human existence and in our struggles to live the Christian life, alone and together, can we begin to discern the way in which the symbols form and express the Christian pattern of affections. We may be profoundly moved by a gesture or by the homily or the music. These are certainly signs of attentiveness and conscious participation. And we do recognize in the reportings various levels of maturity in the apprehension of these elements of word, ritual action, and symbol. But the deeper questions appear only when we allow worshipers to speak about how the liturgy has formed them in deep dispositions over time: in profound gratitude (receiving the world and other human beings as gifts), in hope (even in the face of limits and suffering and death), or in awe and delight of the suffused sense of grace in ordinary meals because one has been present to many Eucharists—some dull, some alive. This is not a call for liturgy that cannot speak to human emotional needs, nor is it a dismissal of the need for "affective immediacy." Rather, it is a call for grounding the formation and expression of human emotion in the deeper reaches of the symbol—in increasing awareness of the "hiddenness" of participation.

The Christian life has depth and resiliency and a liturgical shape. This is so precisely because there is an intrinsic connection between the word and sign-actions of the liturgy and the formation and expression of central emotion capacities in the assembly. Being capable of love, hope, remorse, and gratitude requires much more than the ability to "be moved," though we should never deny the fact that liturgical prayer and the rites may bring intense periods of "feeling" such emotions. Liturgy can be regarded as the community gathered about the word, the font, and the table where the ritual action shapes and expresses human persons in deep emotions that orient us to the mystery of God in creation and in redemption, and in a sense, to the consummation of all things in God. In this sense, liturgy well celebrated should permit us, over time, to refer all things to God and to learn how to intend our lives and the world to God.

There are limits to construing the liturgy exclusively as communal prayer. The whole economy of the rites enacted, as Aidan Kavanagh has pointed out, is more than prayer. Yet in the sense that the liturgy is the ongoing prayer of Jesus Christ in and through the gathered assembly (our ongoing place of communion and dialogue with the divine self-giving) we may sketch briefly how the rites of the Sunday assembly precisely as liturgical prayer can be said to shape and express us in fundamental emotions. "Feeling" such emotions as joy, welcome, remorse, encouragement, and so on is only part of such emotions. Gratitude to God, sorrow for one's sins, compassion, and intentional identification with the suffering are emotions that are ingredients in our judgments and assessments of our lives and our world. Thus, to tell and to hear stories of God and to address God in the vocative of prayer means to undertake a certain way of existing and to behave in certain ways toward others. This is the linkage between the formation of certain emotions in liturgical experience and becoming certain kinds of persons—the formation of character, if you will.

Thus, to thank God, to confess sins, to receive forgiveness, to intercede for others—these are ways of giving and receiving the self in relation to a world. What is done with the words of praise and thanksgiving is part of the meaning of what is said. Insofar as acts of liturgical prayer begin and end in praising and in thanking and blessing God for creation, preservation, and redemption, they constitute a formation in deep emotions. So, gratefulness for life and for the created order as God's gift is part of coming to live gratefully in the world. This is at the heart of Eucharist. It is therefore a cautionary note in the data when relatively few find the participation in the Eucharistic Prayer memorable. Yet the Eucharistic prayer-action, regarded as a whole, still may work at levels of impact below the conscious awareness of thankfulness. At the same time, lack of intention to offer thanks with the presider indicates a low perception of being part of the whole Church's prayer. The more we can enter into the prayer-action of giving thanks, the more likely the formation of deeper, sustained connections between Eucharistic action in the cultus and Eucharistic dispositions in daily living.

But the liturgy of word and Eucharist is more than thanksgiving and praise. It also involves recalling and encountering a memory of a people. In this sense, it is a rite that enacts a complex story. Entering into the memory of Israel and of the New Testament witnesses is also a deepening of awe and wonder. These memories, which come through the readings, the homily, the songs, and the very heart of the Eucharistic action itself, draw together a wide range of emotions and referents. Formation in the word thus forms the assembly in the art of making connections between the symbols and the patterns of experience in life—suffering, aging, struggling with decisions, mixed loyalties, and the like.

Authentic liturgy also brings us to acknowledge who we are in the sight of God. To address God and mean what we say (in word and in gesture) is to recognize our limits and our complicity in evil. In this sense the liturgy explores and continually reveals the difference between who God is and who we are. If praising and thanking are essential to full humanity, so is acknowledgment of sin, of limit, of human ambiguity. This is why such deeper emotional levels as these are available in nearly every dimension of the liturgy, not simply in the penitential rite. The experience of being released, of being freed to live truthfully and without fear or compulsive guilt, is a crucial element in liturgical participation. We did not see as much of this in the data because there were relatively few questions or responses in which the recall of liturgical experience was made in the context of daily life. I suspect, however, that many persons in these parishes could give us valuable insights into how the liturgy does, in fact, shape and express this range of emotional capacity—the capacity for self-examination and for being released to speak the truth in love.

The loss of our experience of the primary symbols in our daily lives—water, bread, light, fire, earth, oil, touch, sounds, silence, gestures—is a loss of our humanity. The diminished sense of biblical memory and connection is a loss of the soil for liturgical participation and growth. So our problem, illustrated amply in the survey, is not that we lack "experiences" in the liturgy. It is that we do not have a strong sense of the discipline and the vulnerability to the *mysterion* of God's self-giving such that depth of experience is possible.

### Concluding Eschatological Hints: Symbol in Liturgy, Liturgy as Symbol

One person in the survey observes: "And I was struck by the Communion lines, . . . the uniqueness of each person going up to receive the Body of Christ. . . . We're all unique with different gifts and different problems but yet we're all one people. I'm struck by that especially when I'm giving Communion, you know, the different shapes and sizes of the hands and the eyes. . . . You'll see someone come up to you and know that they just suffered a death in the family and you'll say that little prayer. . . ." Such is the threshold stuff of moving a personal and social experience into the orbit of the three levels of participation mentioned above. That is, the "personal experience" is in the process of being transformed, honored in its human dimension but taken up into the mystery of the Church and the kingdom.

A Eucharistic example may illuminate these points. In our age the Eucharistic bread presents us with a prophetic icon of a hungry world alongside its received signification as presence and "bread from heaven." So in the context of the liturgy we may be able to regain a heightened discernment of the primary symbolism of meal or banquet, but with a difference. Now a connection is made with the psalmist's "You have prepared a banquet for me [us] in the presence of my enemies." Here the enemies are not foes but those in whose hunger we have been complicit. Augustine's exegesis of the bread asked for in the Lord's Prayer may suddenly come alive (as it may not have in an earlier historical time): We ask for daily bread and for the eschatological bread—and these are mutually interactive. Bread for a hungry world, in which we are called to live responsibly and Eucharistically, and the bread of the kingdom have much to do with each other. This does not reduce the meaning of the bread symbolism to social action; rather, it enriches and renders more powerful God's way with us— with our own mystery, which, as Saint Augustine also reminds us, we receive in the bread. Such a bringing together of meanings and a yoking of cultic and prophetic meanings cannot be a function of our using the symbol to "express" our sensibilities. Rather, such Eucharistic participation is a vulnerable entry together into the concealed range of meanings released in liturgy grounded in the mystery of Church and kingdom.

Alexander Schmemann, of blessed memory, addresses the topic of the organic unity between liturgical participation and the self-giving of God in Christ by urging upon us the essential nature of living liturgy. It is, he claims, the function of liturgy to "bring together, within one symbol, the three levels of the Christian faith and life: the Church, the world, and the Kingdom." It is finally only here, in the *mysterion* of God's presence and action, that the Church may become what it is: the body of Christ and the temple of the Holy Spirit, "the unique SYMBOL, 'bring together,' by bringing to God the world for the life of which God gave his only son."[5]

This, of course, reminds us of the eschatological dimension of all liturgical action. In this sense, any further deepening of liturgical life will depend upon the restoration of a genuinely eschatological appropriation on the part of the assembly of the entire sequence of word and sign-action that constitute the rites of the Church at prayer. It is not a function of preaching alone, though we can certainly ask more biblical depth from our preachers. The recovery of eschatological participation in sign, word, gesture, contemplation, and song depends paradoxically on our learning to distance ourselves from our own cultural assumptions. Liturgy is always culturally embedded and embodied, but the capacity for mystery and for suffering and for delight in the very *doxa* of God comes with having our life experiences broken open and formed by the world of the primary symbol of dying and rising with Christ. At the same time, authentic liturgical participation will challenge the fossilization of symbol by the received tradition. The seeds of prophetic critique of the cultus are borne by the mystery of living encounter with a God who is never guaranteed or encarcerated by our "enjoying the liturgy." Yet still, it is our "duty and delight" always and everywhere to praise God and to listen for God's word, and to receive God's self-giving in the liturgical assembly.

### Notes

1. Joseph Gelineau, *The Liturgy Today and Tomorrow*, trans. Dinah Livingstone (New York/Paramus: Paulist, 1978) 98–99.

2. *Worship: Renewal to Practice* (Washington: The Pastoral Press, 1987) 61–62.

3. See *The Forest of Symbols* (Ithaca: Cornell University Press, 1967), especially 1–47; and "Forms of Symbolic Action: Introduction" in *Forms of Symbolic Action*, ed. Robert F. Spender; Proceedings of the 1969 Annual Spring Meeting of the American Ethnological Society (University of Washington Press, 1969) 3–25.

4. *Liturgy Today and Tomorrow*, 96.

5. "Sacrament: An Orthodox Presentation," in *Gospel and Sacrament*, Oecumenica. (Minneapolis: Augsburg, 1970) 105.

# Reflections on the Study from the Viewpoint of Liturgical History

## Aidan Kavanagh, O.S.B.

Lest the reader think that what follows is entirely dispassionate and objective, I must point out that the dates of the study coincide exactly with my own career as a liturgical scholar. I was sent to Europe by my abbot to begin liturgical studies in 1958, arriving just in time for the death of Pius XII and the accession of John XXIII, who summoned the Second Vatican Council the following year. The next few years were a time of immense ferment, especially in my field of study, as The Constitution on the Sacred Liturgy worked its way through the council; there could have been no finer time to be studying liturgy. We students in Trier were even drawn into making a bit of liturgical history ourselves, even if remotely, since we did a lot of the research that was incorporated into the German bishops' successful bid to have the council approve in principle the reintroduction of Communion under both kinds in the Latin Rite. I took my doctorate at Trier in 1963, having begun to teach already in 1962 and to publish in 1961. I am still at both in 1988, for worse or better, six books and over a hundred essays later, having seen many of the great ones in my field die or retire. I have also had the pleasure of seeing excellent younger colleagues come onto the scene and into the field, some of whom I have the honor of having taught.

But the burden of this essay lies with what has happened to the specifically Roman liturgy during these past twenty-five years. I have probably been too close to the process to be able to see it with total dispassion and objectivity. In the normal course of things, however, one would think that age and experience in one's craft would temper some illusions and deepen candor. I hope that this, at least, will be the case here, and I cannot honestly promise more. Whether I have succeeded will be yours to judge.

My task is to locate the liturgical state reported by the study within the historical stream and to predict what this portends for the future. I suspect that prediction will lie hidden in locating the liturgical state reported by the study within the recent historical evolution of the Roman liturgy. All this is, of course, rife with problems. For one thing, good historians shrink from prediction, as well they might, since they are demonstrably so poor at it. In this, historians are not unlike economists: we can tell people more or less what has happened, but if they believe what we say is going to happen, they do so stupidly. Historians by nature, and I am no exception, excel in fighting the last war.

More to the point, however, is the utter abnormality of the present liturgical state. I am enough of a historian to know that history never really repeats itself. Rather, history proceeds by fits and starts: Long periods of quiescence and status quo are followed by short, intense, and often frenzied periods of evolutionary progress or regress. After the fact, we can usually spot the seeds of such periods lying dormant in the more peaceful periods preceding them—20/20 hindsight for worse or better. It is always hard to see most seeds before they hatch.

Even so, the present liturgical state results from several factors the liturgy has never faced before. For one thing, no ritual system in the history of world religions has ever undergone such substantial changes as those the council precipitated over the past quarter-century, or at so rapid a rate. Just listing the Roman documents of official liturgical changes since the council would fill several fat volumes, and there is no end in sight; nor do the official Roman tabulations exhaust the index of further changes enacted on the linguistic, national, diocesan, and parish levels. Far from suffering from too little change, the present Roman liturgy, if anything, suffers from the abnormality of too much change executed too rapidly. To think otherwise is to ignore social and cultural anthropology.

The results of this suffering do not lie far afield, nor are they difficult to fathom. The main result is confusion among those who cannot keep up with the latest thing, particularly clergy and what are coming to be called "professional laity." If sustained too long, confusion begets demoralization, self-doubt, and finally resignation, a void. All manner of things rush in to fill this void. The study suggests that what has rushed in here are a variety of well-meaning groups (liturgy teams, parish liturgical committees, etc.), who sincerely think of themselves as "helping Father," or as "being Church," or as "experiencing ministry." The expressions of this in the study are consistently genial and benign, but all betray not so much a theological or liturgical rationale as a certain American middle-class attitude, which is more-or-less continually distrustful of expertise, experience, authority, and tradition. Clerical abdication of liturgical and doctrinal responsibility abets this, often receiving in return expressions of support, moral respect, personal affirmation, and a sense of purpose from the groups themselves. Some of this is remarkably arrogant. As a first-year student at Yale recently told a faculty lecturer, "I will let you know when you say something I do not understand."

The worrisome thing about this is not just reduction in necessary clerical self-confidence (surely one factor in the decline of clerical vocations), nor a situation in which when all lead none leads. The worrisome thing is what "committee process" does to the liturgy itself. Responses throughout the study tend to share several eerie committee-type attitudes. For one thing, they regard the liturgy less as a coherent whole than as a series of hermetically sealed actions, in particular what is often called "the rite of gathering the assembly." These units permit respondents to do tactical checklists of what each person's role is supposed to be in them. In the "rite of gathering," for example, ushers and musicians become "ministers of hospitality" who perform services not completely unlike those that Ed McMahon, a minister of hospitality par excellence, does for Johnny Carson; they and others settle, comfort, and whip up the audience for the time when Father and his minions appear for the monologue (the word service and homily) preceding what one respondent characterizes as "magic time," that is, the consecration. Note the gathering-hospitality ethos in the way one parish musician describes the *entire* liturgy of his or her parish (90 percent middle class, 10 percent poor): "Vibrant celebration. Very involved, hospitable community. . . . Celebrant is vivacious, welcoming. . . . The liturgy invites people into community by its warmth and vigor. . . . [We need to] improve upon the rite of gathering the assembly at the beginning of liturgy."

Yet we are told by the study observer that this hospitable community "fences" its altar to practicing adult Roman Catholics just before communion through the words of its vivacious celebrant. Some elements in this vibrant liturgy, we learn, are slide projections that dissolve into each other throughout the rites; prayers and the preface of the Eucharistic Prayer accompanied by piano or guitar; a jug of wine replacing the cup on the altar during the Eucharistic Prayer; the omission of the embolism following the Lord's Prayer, when all hold hands; and giving a "theme" to each liturgy. The study observer estimates that this liturgy is one of high formality, with both its horizontal and vertical dimensions rated equally as 4 out of a possible 5, and that its celebrant dominates it. The impression one has is of a Christian group, largely homogenous and middle class socially, that feels very good about itself, and with a pastor who has a deeper sense of flair than he does of the liturgy of his parish's tradition.

My point is not to belabor or nitpick about style, although one may wonder why *prayers* are always accompanied musically while the reading of the lessons and the homily are not. Rather, my point is to emphasize how very large a role the "rite of gathering" has come to play here and in other parishes reported in the study.

Historically, the *eisodos* or *introit*, entry rites, evolve in direct response to the growing size of churches from the fourth century onward as a complex of movement by clergy and people in off the streets to begin the Eucharistic liturgy. As such, it was a "soft spot," which often defied rigid rubrical stipulations. But this very phenomenology led fairly soon to a general form, which can be seen structurally, and which comes to be commented on by the eighth century. Structurally, the rite is processional and suffused with prayer—psalms and antiphons, litanies, and the oration of the day. The purpose of all this was to put the assembly in a condition to stand before God in a radical act of obedience to him for the life of the world, that is, by accomplishing a *leitourgia*, the present messianism of which is described in Revelation 7.

This traditional and deeply theological attitude is completely changed in the study's liturgical reports. The rite of entry before God for divine service is now a "rite of gathering" whose purpose is hospitality, inviting people into "community." It is often commented on as being consciously calibrated by the interaction of various ministries; ushers, lectors, musicians, and the congregants themselves, who are encouraged to be welcoming, to visit with and introduce themselves to one another both outside and inside the church building right up to the beginning of the service. When the study respondent says that his or her parish needs to "improve upon the rite of gathering the assembly at the beginning of the liturgy," one can see clearly that what is being referred to is no longer an *eisodos* or *introit* of prayer and processional entry but something that precedes and overshadows it, eventually to displace it.

There is no prayer or Godward direction in this new "rite of gathering"; it is a set of activities not ritually very different from the same procedures used when persons of middle-class society gather for any purpose. If it bespeaks any ecclesiology, it seems to be a therapeutic one devoid of any sense of separation from ordinariness; to put it in terms used in the study, the procedure is, in fact, *horizontal* rather than vertical. Indeed, the bustle and noise of gathering would probably rule out *vertical* prayer by individuals before the service. One respondent even notes that there is no time for this after the service, so quickly must the building be locked by maintenance personnel who jingle keys to hurry people out.

But there is one more development apparent in this gathering syndrome deserving mention. One has a sense that the gathering activities people usually undertake naturally and on their own are felt to need organization, even regimentation by corps of ministers. The gathering rite, for all its initial appearance of spontaneity, is, in fact, and no doubt unintentionally, a fairly rigid procedure run by new ministries. One respondent even feels the need to reflect on "the assembly as ministry." This tendency does indeed have precedent in the concept of the Church as servant, but that does not seem to be what is involved here. Or if it is involved, it is given a rather disquieting modern spin in the direction of what one hears so much of these days, namely, ministry as something apart from, often preceding, and even more important than the Church itself. Ministry and "community" are exciting and vivacious; Church is unexciting and a drag on ministerial creativity. Television evangelists and, I am sorry to say, many of our students of divinity at Yale are filled with this attitude. As one of them said to me a few years ago, "I have finally decided what my ministry will be; can you suggest a church that will let me do it?" (Modern "ministries" can become black holes into which whole churches disappear, as in the celebrated cases of Bakker and Swaggart.)

I may be wrong, but the liturgies reported in the study show a *general* tendency to put a premium on the "rites of gathering" at the beginning and end of the liturgy (the social hour afterwards). The liturgy itself, since it has lots of official ecclesiastical rules in it, is a sort of dull in-between time that needs a lot of "brightening up" with slides, dance, drama, a variety of musical instruments and styles, and modestly breathtaking innovations, such as using unauthorized Eucharistic Prayers, by celebrants who are vivacious and, significantly, welcoming.

Without for a moment doubting the good intentions of those who have contributed to this situation, it is perfectly reasonable to question the advisability of much that has been done in view of the future well being of the liturgy of the Roman Rite. Liberality *can* turn into a subtle form of tyranny, manipulating people into approved conformities to social convention rather than liberating them by some sharp-edged counterculturalism. I see very little that is countercultural in the parish liturgies reported in the study. If I may be permitted to say so, I find many of them well-meant examples of what some British sociologists are calling "a slow process of ecclesiastical embourgeoisement [that] has been the main product of the theological hopes of the seventies, an ironic result for a rhetoric of egalitarianism that reached its most ludicrous level of cant amongst radical theologians, whose slant sent many out of the Church."[1] Moreover, "misunderstanding the nature of community and a narrow criterion for evaluating active participation have meant that liturgy is increasingly sanctifying middle-class skills of joining, acting, and proclaiming in public. This has led to the middle class gaining exclusive use of the term 'lay.' "[2] This may be one reason why conservative Fundamentalism has made such serious inroads among those Roman Catholics who are poor and culturally alien to the American middle class, which the liturgies of the study appear to celebrate.

Another reason seems to be a decline in emphasis on the transcendent holiness of God, and consequently on the lack of this quality among worshipers, evident in the liturgies reported in the study. To seek a vertical dimension in these liturgies may not be sufficiently nuanced, for it is one thing to try to generate a "sacral sense" by gearing liturgical rites to symbols held sacred by the middle class, and quite another thing to attend upon the holiness of God, which transcends class, convicts of sin, and strips away illusion. The Macy's Thanksgiving Day parade is full of symbols sacred to the middle class, but they are finally unchristian because the God of Abraham, Isaac, Jacob, Moses, and Jesus the Christ is not that way. One must not trot after false gods and the symbols they endow us with so spectacularly. The awesome holiness of God donates two most fundamental social egalitarianisms, which make Christians cohere in distinctive ways: The first is a sense of communal unworthiness before God; the second is a sense of communal gratitude at being freely and unconditionally raised up and forgiven by God in Christ. Mutual compassion for each other, a frank recognition of sin, thanksgiving for revelation, and prayer for redemption are central attitudes in a community that shares these two radical egalitarianisms. Such a community cannot fail to realize that its worship is entirely messianic according to Revelation 7, where a Lamb slain stands bloody and the cries of the oppressed rise like smoke from beneath the altar of the Lamb before the throne of God.

I find little if any sense of this in the liturgies reported by the study. Rather, I find it constricted, compacted, and emotionally buffered by the middle-class rituals of hospitality and gathering that frame the entire liturgy. As this happens, the transcendental motives for the assembly's solidarity before God in Christ fade and ecclesial dissolution looms. The poor and oppressed are unintentionally forced out, to be remembered only in abstract discussions of social justice after the fact. Just as ominous, the worshiping community itself declines. Recent statistics suggest the decline *at the Sunday liturgy* to be around 30 percent in this country over the last twenty years.[3] Similar flags fly elsewhere: Vocations to ordained ministry are in severe decline, as are vocations to religious orders, some of which are all but out of business (a study of women religious in Quebec reveals that new vocations dropped by over 98 percent between 1961 and 1981, almost as ordinations have in France since 1945). Conversions in England fell from almost sixteen thousand in 1959 to barely five thousand in 1982. Yet vocations to strict monastic orders in France are up by 70 percent over the same general period: Hans Urs von Balthasar noted in 1985 that French contemplative monasteries are full, the seminaries almost empty.[4]

This paradox is only apparent, for a monastery and a seminary, not to say a parish, are different social entities. A monastery of strict observance by nature focuses intensely on God; the freedom it seeks must be won through obedience to myriad rules, and even then the monk's freedom is less immediate than long term, even eschatological, and exercised as often as not in solitude. The clarity of goal is definite, the means to it are clear, and it is supported solidly by the entire group. This is an example of "community" as well as of Victor Turner's category of *communitas*, which any sociologist can recognize and analyze. But a seminary is too transient in its membership and much more varied in its members' intentions to be a community in the same sense. The same might be said of many a modern parish. These factors, if not kept clearly in mind, can lead to equivocal use of "community" when it comes to structuring and accounting for worship in the three different groups. Monastic worship has the same effect advocated by nineteenth-century liturgists as *Gemeinschaft*, namely, binding and strengthening a sense of affiliation, a common identity, from *within*, as one response to the power of the rite as a social activity. This was to intensify internal relationships to the extent that the worshiping group could be, and appear to be, an agent that stood over against the depersonalizing and destabilizing effects of an era of revolutions— political, social, and industrial.

But the sense of "community" current in many worshiping groups today is different. It has become an instrument of edification in its own right, and many of its ideals and techniques are drawn into the wor- shiping group from outside cultures—something that may well impli- cate the Christian group in precisely those cultural elements it should wish to convert, such as political outrage and violence, social divisive- ness, aggressive ideologies pushing a spread of absolutized rights, and questionable incursions into divinely sanctioned relationships.

Liturgical worship that "works" (a verb often used in the study) on the basis of this equivocal sense of "community," it could be ar- gued, is in fact less productive of Christian community than the *Gemein- schaft* sort of liturgy found in strict monastic groups "simply because the former produces mere social relationships, whereas the latter strives to effect a distinctive meaningful element that offers a more clearcut criterion." Such a liturgy as the latter gives "depth and shape to the issue as to what is communal about a liturgical form, and, by adding a distinctive [sacrificial, ecclesially sacerdotal] layer, makes it more than a mere social gathering"[5] that sandwiches "magic time." The other type of liturgy is in imminent danger of producing a "community" that is less fundamentally Christian than it is a middle-class pocket of gentility and self-satisfaction.[6] When this happens, an awareness of the Church as a distinctive counterpoise to the world cannot be main- tained, and the liturgy's authentic task of cultivating a spirit of adora- tion in leading a life toward God must surely falter. As Jungmann remarked long ago, pursuit of this authentic task implies that liturgy, so far from being always freshly created, "requires not only adapta- tion but also, as far as possible, pious conservation and faithful tradi- tion,"[7] precisely those endeavors that the study, with a thunderous silence, reveals to be absent in the parish attitudes it examined.

Having said all this (and there is a great deal more that could and no doubt should be said), I feel it necessary to remind the reader about the opening paragraph of this essay. I am a creature of the Second Vatican Council; my ministry, piety, and academic career have been framed by the council; I am a steadfast advocate of its reforms and will remain so as long as I live. I continue to refuse to have anything to do with the revival of the Tridentine Mass liturgy quite simply because I regard such an attempt as a vast mistake, often well meaning but still mistaken. It is a mistake because the reformed liturgy that has issued from the council is an incomparably more rich, vital, and traditional liturgical settlement in the truly Catholic sense than that of Trent, given its times, ever could have been. If the reforms of the recent council in liturgical worship are not perfect, and if they have suffered from reductionism and misinterpretation, the same happened to the less insightful reforms of Trent during the Counter-Reformation period as well. Even a Mozart concerto can be badly played.

I well remember the doing of Tridentine liturgy. Silent Masses in parishes, few if any Communions (almost *never* when the Mass was sung), doubts about whether the faithful were even allowed to make the responses, the numbing proliferation of private Masses in religious houses, ugly vestments, and good-night hymns to the Little White Guest locked up for the night in our tabernacles. Those were the days when the main liturgical rubric was minimalism, piety was something else, and liturgy had nothing theological about it except in the form and matter required for the valid confection of the sacraments. Celebrating clergy had to recite the liturgy's sung parts; it was doubtful whether they were allowed to sing them, even along with the choir. The people almost never sang except at novenas and Benediction of the Blessed Sacrament, which were often more festive than the Mass of the day. The Tridentine liturgy was, by the twentieth century, a liturgy filled with non sequitur. It was rarely done well, but contained enough late medieval and baroque elements (buskins, gauntlets, a seventh altar candle when ordinaries celebrated, vesting at the altar, rolled-up chasubles called broad stoles worn by deacons and subdeacons during Lent, maniples, and so on) to intrigue those with recondite tendencies. Serious theologians and hardheaded pastors, of course, regarded this sort of thing as a playground for aesthetes or as little more than "God's table manners." Once between trains in Chicago I attended a solemn requiem High Mass in a famous local church that lasted barely fifteen minutes, and it was all sung, including the lengthy *Dies irae*.

So I harbor no illusions about the "old liturgy" and the way we used it. The rubrics, symbols, and the chant (rarely heard in parishes) were regularly murdered. Seminarians were never taught how to preside at worship, only how to confect a sacrament validly and to fulfill minimally the obligation of reading the Divine Office daily according to canon law's inscrutable ways of determining time—not the *opus dei*, but the *onus diei*.

But despite what all this may have lacked, it did have one thing that was galvanizing on clergy and people sufficient to be remarked on in awe even by unsympathetic outsiders. It was *discipline*. Indeed, it could be argued that the Tridentine liturgy, which prevailed throughout the Counter-Reformation until twenty-five years ago, was less a system of worship than it was a system of discipline that had soaked into and affected every aspect of Catholic life. If the liturgical forms themselves were perhaps qualitatively not very good, often even unintelligible on their own merits, the sense of *obligation* to them was enough to override doubts about specifics and to create a remarkable egalitarianism that embraced us all, uniting us to common purpose. A Mass fumbled through by a senseless celebrant with all the panache of Woody Allen trying to seduce Mae West was still the Mass; for that we kissed his hands but rarely invited him home to dinner. I have seen philosopher and charwoman kneeling side by side at such Masses; she with her Missal, he with his rosary, both of them offering up their priest to God along with their love and sins.

Discipline and a sense of obligation made this remarkably functional egalitarianism possible. Even more significant, perhaps, it made humor unavoidable. For since humor is the detection of incongruity, it was immediately clear to all, given the clear-cut discipline of the rites themselves, when something incongruous had occurred, and it often took very little to reduce a parish congregation or a monastic choir to hilarity. As when my abbot knocked off his miter with a huge mop-like aspergil while sprinkling our new fire truck with holy water during a downpour. And not a few people noticed that when Cardinal Spellman got dressed up to celebrate pontifical High Mass, it was eerily like watching the Infant of Prague come to life, but an Infant with whom it was advisable not to trifle. Discipline and obligation laid a heavy burden but at the same time assured the catharsis and intense social bonding of glee in the detection of clearly demarcated incongruities. We seem, oddly, to have been rather less solemn about ourselves then than we are now, and I have no doubt that the liturgy had a lot to do with it.

I also am beginning to think that we were, on the whole, healthier as Church then than we are now. There were more converts then,

Masses were generally well attended, seminaries and religious houses were full, there was an esprit assured by common practices such as Friday abstinence and fasting before Communion; roles were clear. American Catholicism was a bit corrupt, somewhat crazy, and not a little magnificent. In the summers at Notre Dame during the fifties and sixties it charmed the socks off great European scholars such as Jungmann, Daniélou, Bouyer, Mohrmann, Fischer, and others who were imported to lecture to us on liturgy and its implications. National Liturgical Weeks filled arenas with thousands upon thousands of clergy and laity (rarely bishops) every summer. The Mass and its language were the same discipline and obligation in Saigon as in Paris, Rome, Capetown, and Dubuque; to this all had access, and bore up under, just as they did at home. We felt closer, therefore, to each other in our suffering.

This is much less the case today. The old discipline and its egalitarian sense of obligation is now replaced by local options often generated by committees made up of clergy and semiprofessional laypersons who represent largely middle-class values and techniques of short-term joining and therapy, which may often be problematic for the poorer classes and disdained by the upper classes. A kind of humorless symbol mongering often seems to result from this, buffering or even suffocating the fundamental sacramental reality at the core of the rite—the sacrifice of thanksgiving to God in Christ being transmuted into some kind of cultural high tea followed by seminars on social justice, world hunger, or how we are and are not permitted to speak of God in brave new ways. Such issues, no less than liturgical form and sacramental symbolism, are very important indeed. They are also *very* complex, require high discipline and competence, and are trivialized by simplistic reductionism when they fall into the hands of the undisciplined and incompetent. One sees this in the seriously put and well-intentioned question of whether the Eucharist may even be celebrated in a world where genocides, hunger, and injustice abide. It may be argued that such a world needs the Eucharist all the more; but *not* the sort of Eucharist that celebrates middle-class values and techniques that buffer the fundamental sacramental reality at the core of the rite. (I am haunted by the observation of one respondent in the study that his or her parish in one year spent $70,000 on music but only $3,000 on religious education.) Nor can one overlook the fact that the liturgy is not geared to have direct causal results on complex and long-term social problems. The liturgy, while laced with prophecy, is itself a poor prophet; prophets prophesy best in other forums. The liturgy, while filled with the messianic vision of a new heaven and new earth which it celebrates, is itself not an agency of social services; other groups do this better in other forums.

What historic liturgical systems have been meant to do is to manifest the root metaphor of the body of Christ *on* the table and *around* the table by enculturating this metaphor in accessible ways, thereby transforming the way in which the social body of the Church views and engages the entire cosmos. Historic liturgies have done this sometimes better, sometimes worse, but they have always done it *sub specie aeternitatis*, bringing whatever elements they appropriated from the culture, together with the culture itself in all its aspects, beneath the criteria of God's Word speaking in Scripture, in the incarnation, and in the Church's apostolic tradition. What this Word has always told those who celebrate liturgy is that the Holy One in whose presence they stand is pleased to have them stand there precisely because of their sin, which merited so great a redeemer, and that because of this they have here no abiding city. Their home is with God in Christ, who reveals his Father just as the Holy Spirit reveals him to them as the Christ of God. Their liturgical worship belongs to these Three, who allow us to take our unmerited and gratuitously given part in it, and it discomfits us as it comforts. In no way must it confirm us in our illusions—that this liturgy belongs to us, or our social class, or our culture, or our world; that we are without sin; that our salvation is sure in spite of what we do; that our prognosis is only progress; that our city will abide; that our glands preside; that more education has all the answers. A "divine liturgy" is a countercultural tornado, and we do it not for ourselves, or the parish, or the Church, but for the life of the world.

Part of my task was to locate the state of liturgy reported in the study within the historical stream. This is almost impossible to do, as I noted, because of the unique quantity and rapidity of the reforms that produced this liturgy over the past twenty-five years. It is too early to document whether what we are doing with what has been produced represents progress or regress. Yet some symptoms give plausibility to the intuition that the liturgical *usage* reported in the study is problematic.

For one thing, there is an unbearable lightness of doctrine evident in the uses of the reformed rite itself. What doctrine there is seems to center on "community" and "ministry," both ritually defined in middle-class categories, worrisomely to the unintended exclusion of the less affluent classes. For another thing, where deeply traditional doctrine has receded (doctrine touching the holiness of God and the sinfulness of humankind), a sort of cultural symbol mongering seems to have taken its place along with attempts to produce approved "experiences" of dance, music, ministry, community, drama, and so on. In this, newfound freedom in liturgical discipline may be imperceptibly modulating into new forms of constraint aimed at producing some kind of typical middle-class Catholic, a development that will reduce the range of usable symbols no less than the sorts of persons such a "community" will allow to belong to it.

For a final thing, there seems to be little depth to the liturgies as reported. It is as though their celebrants expect various meanings to be completely yielded up on the doing of each ritual and to be completely absorbed in an approved manner by each participant. But true art and symbolism always leave great residues of meaning that can never be exhausted in any one performance. These great residues are what furnish the ongoing reservoir of meaning, which people of all classes and vocations must be free to return to at any time, whether inside or outside the time of performance. The use of rites and symbols in the liturgies reported by the study are not like this; they are too neat, tidy, and almost automatically functional; they are expected to "work," and work now. They are not like sonnets, but like jingles; not like Bach's *Mass in B Minor*, but like Muzak; not like an icon, but like an ad in a glossy magazine; not like a well-crafted country church or a great cathedral such as Chartres, but like a shopping mall. In trying to avoid some sort of elitism, one suspects, those who celebrate the liturgies reported in the study appear to have invented a new elitism of rituals and symbols out of which has departed meaning residue, leaving little on which worshipers might sustain their prayer and contemplation. Yet the liturgy's power lies precisely in this residue, and if people do not find it there, they will seek it elsewhere.

The other part of my task was to predict the future of such a liturgy. If (and it is a very big if) my intuition of symptoms is correct, I suspect that this liturgical usage will produce a Church that will gradually become both more sensitive and more irrelevant, not necessarily less numerous but probably so. For why should people go to such a liturgy in order to be affirmed in values that are at least as well celebrated elsewhere without the vaguely discomforting occasional word of the gospel? Many liberal Protestant Churches have long gone in this direction and now find themselves in very steep decline indeed. Ac-

cording to a recent Gallup poll prepared for twenty-two religious or-
ganizations and their National Festival of Evangelism in Chicago in
August 1988, while belief in Jesus Christ's divinity is held by 84 percent of the American people, over 75 percent thought that ''a person
can be a good Christian or Jew even if he or she does not attend a
church or synagogue.'' Also, 80 percent said that ''a person should
arrive at his or her religious beliefs independent of any church or synagogue,'' and the poll showed little difference of opinion between
American Protestants and Catholics.

The conclusion is clear: Churches are slowly losing their influence
with believers, whose membership in them has declined from 1978 by
17 million: put negatively, 61 million did not belong then, 78 million
do not belong now. It may well be that one factor in this is that the
sort of worship that goes on in the churches is slowly easing church
members into largely middle-class American civil religion apart from
the Church and its worship assemblies.[8] It is quite clear that liberal
groups, both civil and ecclesiastical, are not nearly so productive of
*membership* as are their conservative counterparts, both here and around
the world. If a liturgical assembly is to survive, much less be powerful
enough to do fundamental good in the world, it must come to terms
with these relentless statistics. One must beware lest, as already noted,
the Church dissolve into exciting and vivacious ministries whose main
purpose is to gather people for hospitality and ''magic time,'' and
whose social bonding patterns are weak or vanishing.

As Newman said:

> What is the world's religion now? It has taken the brighter side of the
> Gospel—its tidings of comfort, its precepts of love; all darker, deeper
> views of man's condition and prospects being comparatively forgot-
> ten. This is the religion natural to a civilized age. . . .
>
> New objects in religion, new systems and plans, new doctrines,
> new preachers, are necessary to satisfy that craving which the . . .
> spread of knowledge has created. The mind becomes morbidly sensi-
> tive and fastidious; dissatisfied with things as they are, desirous of
> change as such, as if the alteration must of itself be a relief.[9]

What Newman said over a hundred years ago had been said already in greater detail by the author of the Letter to the Galatians. It
is a lesson we must all relearn in every generation, even as we rejoice
in the reforms of our worship over the past twenty-five years. I have
been and remain a strong advocate of those reforms. But in what we

often make of them I must be an even stronger advocate of the gospel of Jesus Christ as it continues to be received through the apostolic tradition and teaching of his Church. I commend the thought that one cannot go far wrong by staying close to that gospel, that tradition, and that teaching, both now and in the years to come.

### Notes

1. Kieran Flanagan, "Resacralizing the Liturgy," *New Blackfriars* 68 (1987) 64.

2. Flanagan, "Resacralizing the Liturgy," 65.

3. See, e.g., The Diocese of Columbus, Ohio, *Liturgical Apostolate* 20:2 (1984) 11.

4. *L'heure de l'Eglise* (Paris, 1986) 36-37, quoted in Flanagan, "Resacralizing the Liturgy," 70.

5. Flanagan, "Resacralizing the Liturgy," 72.

6. See A. Archer, *The Two Catholic Churches: A Study in Oppression* (London, 1986) 211-216.

7. *Pastoral Liturgy* (London 1962) 338 and 372.

8. I am aware of several recent studies that generally concur: Nathan Mitchell, "Liturgical Education in Roman Catholic Seminaries: A Report and an Appraisal," *Worship* 54 (1980) 129-157, especially 146-152; Mark Searle, "The Notre Dame Study of Catholic Parish Life," *Worship* 60 (1986) 312-333, especially 333; M. Francis Mannion, "Liturgy and the Present Crisis of Culture," *Worship* 62 (1988) 98-123. Searle and Mannion refer to Robert N. Bellah and others, *Habits of the Heart: Individualism and Commitment in American Life* (New York, 1985).

9. John Henry Newman, "The Religion of the Day," in *Parochial and Plain Sermons* (1825-1843) 331 and 313.

# Pastoral Liturgical Reflections on the Study

*John F. Baldovin, S.J.*

Recent scholarly investigation has shown that in the history of the Church, councils are only considered ecumenical after they have been received by the Church at large. A convenient example is the Council of Chalcedon (451), considered by the Roman and Orthodox Churches as the fourth ecumenical council, but of course not considered thus by Churches that have been called Monophysite. Today the Second Vatican Council is still in the process of reception by the Church. The survey *Liturgical Renewal 1963–1988* shows, I think, that this reception process is well along. In fact, in terms of liturgical renewal the council's efforts have achieved a remarkable level of acceptance except among the smallest minority. It is my intention here to reflect on this renewal in terms of pastoral liturgical theology.

What is the task of the liturgical theologian? Simply put, it is to reflect in a coherent fashion on the Church's experience of public prayer and to do this with serious attention to Scripture, history, and the contemporary experience of the Church. The pastoral liturgical theologian must do this with a keen eye to the social-psychological conditions that obtain in any particular culture or era. Theology, after all, is always an act of interpretation and as such is inevitably governed by the interpreter's background, life situation, blindspots, and limitations of perspective. This is why theology's task is never complete, never a final synthesis of all that can be said of God and God's relation to the world. The fact that Christian faith keeps on being experienced in different times and different places forces us to reflect anew on the faith in general and on its particular aspects as well.

Nowhere is this more true than in the field of liturgy, affected as it is by cultural conditions, for the Church's worship is not a set of texts and rubrics written down in books but the living experience of Christian assemblies. Therefore, as with drama, one can learn a great deal from the script, but true appreciation of liturgy as an event can come only with the experience of the play (liturgy) itself.

*Liturgical Renewal 1963–1988* provides us with an opportunity to reflect on the state of the post–Vatican II Roman Catholic liturgy as it is experienced in fifteen middle-class American parishes concerned with renewal. The limitations of the data restricted as they are to parishes that have made a serious effort at renewal should be obvious. It is also clear that the survey makes no pretense at being scientific in the sociological sense. It seems to me, however, on the basis of my own experience with a variety of parishes around the country, that this survey, impressionistic as it is, does provide an opportunity to consider the major pastoral-theological issues surrounding liturgy today. Therefore, in what follows I propose to do the following: first, to ask the formal question What is the place of "experience" in liturgical theology?, second, to reflect on the various sacramental images that the survey surfaces, and finally, to discuss three fundamental issues in pastoral practice that the survey suggests.

### The Place of "Experience" in Liturgical Theology

It is not too bold to say that today theology in general and with it liturgical theology are in the midst of a paradigm shift—from a classical world view to one that can be characterized as "modern." Some are even willing to argue that theology, having exhausted the modern paradigm, is shifting to one that can be designated "postmodern."[1] In any case, the shift that is taking place can adequately be described as moving from a model of ahistorical truths enshrined in a fundamentally unchanging tradition to the priority of experience in evaluating theological claims. The former model is characteristic of Scholastic theology, while the latter "turn to the subject" (to employ a phrase of Bernard Lonergan) is characteristic of theologians after Kant, beginning with Schleiermacher.

One can find the shift I am describing very well exemplified in two different styles of sacramental theology. The classic form relies first and foremost on the data provided by the doctrinal (even more than the scriptural) tradition, for example in Bernard Leeming's *Principles of Sacramental Theology*.[2] This older style of sacramental theology neatly distinguishes the form and content of liturgical celebration. It is as if sacraments were sacred formulas, actions, and things encased in a changeable liturgy that has little or no bearing on the reality of the sacrament itself. One of the major results of the liturgical reform, especially in the twentieth century, has been the realization that the form of the liturgy (its celebration) and the content of the sacraments are inseparable.

The modern form has taken two directions. The first reflects on sacraments primarily on the basis of a phenomenology of human experience, as in Bernard Cooke's *Sacraments and Sacramentality*.[3] This style of sacramental theology, thoroughly in tune with the renewal of theology in general, represents a significant advance over a "dogmatic" method that tends to remain mired in the disputes of the past, especially those of the sixteenth-century Reformation. But the second direction is even more important for our purposes. This style of sacramental theology is more appropriately called liturgical theology, for it attends not only to phenomenological data and to the findings of the human sciences, but it also analyzes the text and actions of various liturgical celebrations. Raymond Vaillancourt's *Toward a Renewal of Sacramental Theology*[4] is an example of this effort. One should mention here the very different attempts of Aidan Kavanagh, David Power, and Robert Taft in this regard.[5] Finally the excellent series *Alternative Futures for Worship*[6] has provided us with the findings of the human sciences combined with the traditional concerns of sacramental theology and an analysis of liturgical celebration.

Underlying both of these modern views is a wider concept of sacramentality made popular by Karl Rahner, who understands the Church to be the basic sacrament,[7] and Edward Schillebeeckx, who sees Christ as the primordial sacrament.[8] In other words, the process of symbolization (in theological terms, "sacramentality") is not a mere appendage to the Christian experience of faith but rather an integral dimension of all human knowing and acting.[9]

I would want to argue that this modern shift is a necessary correction of a theology that in a one-sided way emphasized extrinsic concerns, that is, based itself on views of positive commands by God that are not grounded sufficiently in an understanding of the human that can make sense to contemporary human beings. For better or worse,[10] theology in all of its forms must take an anthropological starting point today. This criterion poses an important challenge to the liturgical theologian, for, in my opinion, contemporary liturgical scholarship has placed too high a value on a relatively uncritical recovery of liturgical forms of the past. Two examples will suffice to make my point. The current Order for the Roman Catholic Eucharist is clearly a copy of the seventh-century *Ordo Romanus primus*—without that document's frills of imperial-ecclesiastical court etiquette—undoubtedly an advance over the "medieval low Mass" model operative prior to Vatican II, but still only one time-conditioned model for what might be possible in the ritualization of the Roman Catholic Eucharist. In the area of initiation the RCIA is clearly modeled on the early third-century *Apostolic Tradition* of Hippolytus, a somewhat problematic document that we cannot even be sure was ever really used. Liturgical theologians, myself included, have yet to develop a critical hermeneutic for the study of liturgical history.[11]

The lack of a developed criteriology for liturgical history is paralleled by some assumptions that are implicit in the use of experiential data—a matter on which I wish to focus for the remainder of this section. In his provocative recent book, *The Nature of Doctrine: Religion and Theology in a Post Liberal Age*,[12] George Lindbeck has questioned the operative definitions of religion that underlie so much of contemporary theology and its theories of doctrine. While I must admit that Lindbeck's theory of doctrine does present some problems, his analysis of the three models employed by students of religion strikes right at the heart of the relation between experience and theology.

The first model is named "cognitivist" or "propositionalist" and is characteristic of the view of traditional orthodoxy. It treats the language of the truth claims of a particular religion in realist or objective fashion. The Enlightenment and especially Kant's first philosophical critique have made this a problematic (if not terribly unpopular) view of religion and its function.

The second model Lindbeck terms "experiential" or "expressivist." The fundamental presupposition of this model is a universal religious experience that is merely expressed in different ways by diverse religious faiths. In the field of the study of religion it had its origins in Schleiermacher's "feeling of absolute dependence" and has had its heirs among most of the major theologians popular in the twentieth century—Paul Tillich, Rudolf Bultmann, Langdon Gilkey, to name but a few. It has also been employed by students of religion in general, for example Rudolf Otto and Mircea Eliade.[13] Lindbeck finds that the experiential or expressivist approach fails to appreciate that there is no one common religious experience universal to humankind in general and for this reason is inadequate. A variation on both of these first two models can be discerned in the theologies of Karl Rahner and Bernard Lonergan, who for Lindbeck combine the cognitivist and experientialist approaches.

As is usual in the case of typologies, the last given, the cultural-linguistic model, is the author's favorite. This postliberal model "places emphasis on those respects in which religions resemble languages together with their correlative forms of life and are thus similar to cultures—that is, as idioms for the construction of reality and the living of life."[14] Proponents of this understanding of religion can be found in the school of thought called the sociology of knowledge (Peter Berger, Thomas Luckmann) as well as in the thought of Karl Marx, Emile Durkheim, Max Weber, Clifford Geertz, Ninian Smart, and (the later) Ludwig Wittgenstein.

The parallel between Lindbeck's cultural-linguistic model and the nature of liturgy suggests that we are formed by liturgy just as much as (or perhaps even more than) we form it; that is to say, liturgy, like religion, is not merely the product of our "extraliturgical" or "preliturgical" experience but, rather, shapes all of our experience. It is one of the religious ways that we achieve our most authentic identity.

The implications for the use of the category "experiential" in contemporary liturgical theology are profound indeed. Like any living language liturgy develops and changes. Its "vocabulary" is expanded; new "metaphors" are added to it; new "patterns of speech" emerge. And, as with language, the novel aspects of liturgy are the products of a certain genius, a gift for insight into the nature of the world. But we tend to forget that, like speaking a language, liturgy is something we learn. It is not the "expressive" product of our manipulation—something that we have thought up.

And so, while it would be foolish to discount the element of experience in contemporary liturgy and to fail to be attentive to the needs of worshipers, at the same time it would be equally foolish to neglect the formative powers of the symbols and rituals that go to make up Christian worship. This concern is all the more pressing given the "subjectivist" bias of our age.[15] Never before in the history of the world have so many people been so deeply concerned about how they feel. Never before have they been so vocal about it. And, more important, never before have so many been so concerned to listen to them. This is not to say that the experiential data provided by the survey is not significant, but rather that it must be sifted in a critical way. Thus, when interviewees report that such and such an aspect of the liturgy was meaningful for them, we must ask, just what does "meaningful" mean here? It has long been my suspicion that what is truly meaningful about liturgy is experienced on a very subtle level and is not accessible for immediate articulation.

So, when people complain that certain aspects of the liturgy are boring or hold no interest for them, we should be wary about coming to the rapid conclusion that these have no meaning.[16] In other words, attentiveness and meaning are not necessarily synonymous. We are seldom attentive to the patterns that are most formative of our lives. When "they are out of whack" some form of analysis (or even psychoanalysis) is called for to bring them to our conscious attention, but normally these patterns work their subtle effects without much awareness on our part. I am suggesting that liturgy is one of those patterns and that therefore the temptation to constant change that seems to be the constant agenda of so many liturgical planners should be avoided.

If experience is an ambiguous criterion on which to build a liturgical theology, what should characterize the kind of critical theology that is called for? A balance of three factors: the rule of prayer, the rule of faith, and the rule of practice. In recent years much effort has gone into reflecting on the traditional axiom *lex orandi, lex credendi,* or the intimate connection between the rule of prayer and the rule of faith. In its original formulation, of course, the principle stated that "the rule of prayer grounds the rule of faith,"[17] but in practice the axiom has been far more dialogical. What Christians believe and how they pray have always affected each other. In fact, as Maurice Wiles has demonstrated, it was actually personal piety more than official liturgical formulations that affected the development of Trinitarian and Christological doctrines in the fourth and fifth centuries.[18] Today, however, we are becoming more and more sensitive to the need for adding a third aspect to the axiomatic *lex orandi, lex credendi,* namely, *lex agendi,* the rule of practice.[19] What kind of (moral) activity is characteristic of people of faith, people who have been formed by liturgical worship? If no notable difference can be discerned on the level of Christian living, then one must ask if there is any significance at all to what goes on in worship or in the faith life of the Church.

### Sacramental Images

Let us turn now more directly to the survey itself and some of the issues it raises for liturgical theology in the wake of the council. Perhaps most significant are the sacramental images that surface in the course of the descriptions of the Sunday liturgies and the follow-up interviews. In an impressionistic survey of this sort it would be impossible to name, with any scientific exactitude precisely, what people are saying is sacramental. But certain words and phrases are repeated with some frequency and point, I think, to a general sacramental vision. The words are "warmth," "comfortable," "community," "to feel good," "closeness," and "togetherness."

These words and phrases speak volumes about the needs and yearnings of contemporary middle-class Americans. It is fairly obvious that many people intensely desire a feeling of belonging and togetherness and that they are happy with liturgy when it provides that feeling. One index of the importance of the need for a feeling of togetherness is the percentage of people in the survey who received Communion from the cup. As Gordon Lathrop has perceptively stated in a recent essay on AIDS and the cup, reluctance to receive from a common cup probably has more to do with the power of the symbolic sharing communicated by this action than with germs or viruses.[20] On balance, the parishes surveyed seem to be doing very well in communicating a sense of true community, given the number of people who received from the cup at the liturgies observed.

The question this raises for sacramental imagery is not whether people ought to feel this way or whether they ought to bring an expectation of community and intimacy to liturgy but how precisely does and should liturgy fulfill this need. The first thing that must be said is that liturgy cannot make up for the lack of community in other dimensions of life.

One of the most significant dangers of the contemporary renewal of liturgical life is the overblown expectations that many people (including liturgists) tend to bring to it. To expect liturgy to create a community that does not otherwise exist in any way, shape, or form is to confuse symbolic or ritual activity with daily life. These are inseparably interrelated, but they are not interchangeable. Of course, one of the functions of ritual activity is to enhance community identity, but, as we say, "grace builds on nature"—community is not created out of whole cloth. The social isolation that we and so many of our contemporaries experience poses one of the most difficult challenges to our appreciation of sacramentality. One of the results is that people are tempted to look to liturgy for immediate gratification and that when communal identity is accentuated to such a degree, the element of mission is underemphasized. Overattention to intimacy and warmth also inhibits worshipers from experiencing sacramental action as God's gift rather than their own creation. Part and parcel of the overblown expectations that are brought to worship is the perverse notion that worship is somehow our good idea in the first place. It isn't, of course, for it is the result of the prompting of the Spirit—a much neglected aspect of liturgical theology in Western Christianity. There is very little sense in the survey of the Church as *ekklesia*—an assembly of human beings that has been convoked by God.

Given the search for intimacy and community as one of the primary modes of God's presence with us—at least as this is felt by contemporary worshipers—what does the survey tell us about how people understand the Eucharist? The reactions of the people interviewed point to a certain limitation on the meaning of the Eucharist. Contemporary reflection on the nature of symbolic activity has taught us that symbols are never reduced to simple univocal meanings without suffering a loss of much of their power to evoke feeling, thought, and action.[21] The richness of multiple meaning involved in the celebration of the Eucharist is evoked by the five meanings named in the "Eucharist" section of the World Council of Churches' ecumenical convergence document, *Baptism, Eucharist, and Ministry* (the *Lima Document*). These five fundamental aspects of the Eucharist are thanksgiving to the Father, anamnesis or memorial of Christ, invocation of the Holy Spirit, Communion of the faithful, and meal of the kingdom.[22] Of these five meanings, only the fourth, Communion of the faithful, predominates in the responses of the survey.

The emphasis on Communion and community and on the fellowship-meal dimension of the Eucharist is indeed a great and long-overdue gain for Roman Catholics. As I have said, these aspects of liturgical celebration hold an appeal for today's Catholics. Doubtless, too, each era will concentrate on one or another facet of the rich meaning of Eucharistic celebration. The challenge to liturgical theologians (and to liturgical planners) is to appreciate this contemporary gain in the worship life of Catholics and at the same time to preserve and reflect upon the other vital dimensions of the Eucharist as well.

All of this is not to say that people do not appreciate the presence of Christ in the Eucharistic elements of bread and wine. Despite their clear inattention to the Eucharistic Prayer (a subject we will return to), a deeply ingrained sense of the presence of Christ in the elements endures. For example, a number of people, when asked about the Eucharistic Prayer, were rather embarrassed that they "blanked out" during it, since they knew it contained the "consecration." One person put it this way when asked what came next after the preparation of the gifts and table: "After this we have the transubstantiation." That the sophisticated language of Scholastic theology and the Catholic doctrinal tradition has slipped into a description of what happens in the course of the Eucharist is an index of how thoroughly Catholics have been trained to appreciate Christ's presence in the Eucharistic elements.

People's reactions to the liturgy thus contain an interesting combination of the old and the new. A rather narrow concentration of the presence of Christ in the transformed bread and wine coexists happily within a more deeply felt framework of the Communion meal. The challenge for liturgists (both scholars and practitioners) is to help people, through catechesis and above all through liturgical celebration, to make the connections between the various dimensions of the Eucharist—between the presence of Christ in the assembly, the word, the ministers, and the elements themselves. I am not suggesting that people need to be taught technical terms like *anamnesis, eucharistia,* or *berakah,* but rather that the very structure and dramatic presentation of the liturgy ought to help them make these connections on a deeply felt level. For example, appreciating the vertical and horizontal dimensions of participating in Communion (that we are bonded with one another as we commune with Christ) ought to lead people to the recognition that the Eucharist is an anticipatory sign of the coming kingdom of God's justice and peace and therefore to the daily living out of the justice and peace that witness to that kingdom. Clearly, in the parishes that are most serious about liturgical renewal, these kinds of connections are being made.

I have spent a good deal of time trying to analyze why I was so perturbed by the fact that the majority of the participant-interviewees mentioned the exchange of peace and/or holding hands at the Lord's Prayer as the high point of the Sunday Eucharistic liturgy. These are not bad things in themselves. As a matter of fact, they are rather healthy signs that people (for the most part) want to worship together and not in splendid isolation. Clearly, emphasizing the communal dimension of Eucharist has made its mark on at least a significant portion of Catholic worshipers. Clearly, people have been profoundly influenced by the RCIA, which, in my opinion, acts as a kind of subtext for the whole of the survey. At the same time, however, we need to ask whether the more transcendent and the more challenging aspects of the Eucharist, as outlined in the *Lima Document*, need to be heeded. It is clear to me that they do.

Part of the effort to expand the sacramental images that appeal to people in the liturgy must also involve the way liturgical actions, people, and things are described. I noted that the survey questioners consistently employed the term "celebrant" rather than "presider." In this practice they are well within the usage that has been enshrined in Vatican II's Constitution on the Sacred Liturgy as well as the General Instruction on the Roman Missal. But experience of the liturgical renewal has made us aware that the assembly is the true celebrant of the liturgy—the assembly, that is, in Christ. The presider plays a necessary but limited and well-defined role in the celebration.[23] This is not a matter of quibbling about technical terms; words do make a difference in how people conceive reality. Persistence in using misleading words encourages persistence in a way of thinking that most contemporary students of the liturgy, myself included, consider misguided. Another example is the use of the term "offertory" or the phrase "offertory procession." Once again this corresponds to official usage, at least with regard to the chant that accompanies this portion of the celebration. Once again, it is not quibbling over niceties to suggest that "offertory" connotes an independent action, independent, that is, of the Eucharistic Prayer. Presentation of the gifts and/or preparation of the gifts and table, while verbally a bit more awkward, connote much better the preparatory nature of this ritual action (and might even someday have the salutary effect of helping presiders to be attentive to the rubrics of the Sacramentary when they direct an action of placing the gifts rather than offering them up). Gender-inclusive language does not exhaust the areas of linguistic carefulness in contemporary liturgy.

### Issues for Pastoral Reflection

In addition to the more fundamental questions of experience as a category for liturgical theology and sacramental imagery, I want to discuss three areas that call for pastoral reflection. The first two of these areas seem to me the more pressing.

### 1. Eucharistic Prayer

It can be stated rather directly and with little doubt that with the possible exception of its sung acclamations, the Eucharistic Prayer is experienced by participants in this survey as the dullest part of the Eucharistic liturgy. On one level, given what was said in the first section of this essay about levels of experience being deeper than the superficially conscious, this need not be terribly troubling. People do have a native sense of the importance of the Eucharistic Prayer even if they do not attend to it. On another level, however, we must ask, Must it be *so* boring? After all, the General Instruction on the Roman Missal states unequivocally that the Eucharistic Prayer is the "center and high point" of the celebration.[24] However true this may be theologically, it is certainly not the case experientially.

It could be the case that the long overdue focus on Communion has made the Eucharistic Prayer seem less important in the minds of Catholic worshipers. And I would even be willing to argue the correctness of that perception—primacy in theory as in practice belong to the culminating moment of the Eucharistic action, the sharing of Communion. Yet, surely the articulation of the action itself deserves better than to be practically ignored.

That the Eucharistic Prayer is very little attended to points, in my opinion, to a weakness in the reformed *Ordo* of the Roman Eucharist. From the blessing formulas at the preparation of the gifts to the invitation to Communion, there are simply too many words, too many prayers. In part, this is a result of the compromises that resulted from adopting the *Ordo Romanus primus* as well as several medieval developments as the model of the Eucharistic rite. Here we would do well to learn from the current order of the Eucharist of the Episcopal *Book of Common Prayer* of 1979 or the *Lutheran Book of Worship* of 1978, where the Eucharistic Prayer can stand out in the Eucharistic action because it is not hedged in by other prayers. Were I to be asked to rewrite this part of the liturgy, I would suggest dropping the blessing formulas, the "Pray brothers and sisters" and its response, the prayer over the gifts, the embolism after the Lord's Prayer, and the prayer preceding the greeting of peace, not to mention the private prayers of the presider, which inevitably get spoken aloud contrary once again to the directions in the rubrics. Perhaps this suggestion reflects my penchant for "minimalist" music, but I am convinced that were this suggestion taken, nothing important would be lost in the liturgy—*a fortiori* the Eucharistic Prayer could stand out as *the* central prayer of the celebration.

Merely highlighting the Eucharistic Prayer by deleting what ends up seeming like incessant chatter is not sufficient. The lack of attention given to the Eucharistic Prayer also implies that it is not being prayed well. It is prayed without passion, without a sense of its importance. One often has the sense that a variable preface and particular Eucharistic Prayer are not chosen so much for their connection to the Liturgy of the Word as for convenience or simply because they have not been used for a while. Perhaps public prayer is a lost art; perhaps presiders need to be convinced that if they do not passionately mean what they say when they pray the Eucharistic Prayer, no one will listen.

A final recommendation with regard to the Eucharistic Prayer: People must be invited to active listening. Having worshipers kneel during the prayer not only reinforces a chasm between "celebrant" and assembly, it invites them to be passive. Active participation does not mean that everyone needs to do everything in the liturgy, as Ralph Keifer pointed out so well some time ago, [25] but it does mean that they should be given cues to listen actively. Only the posture of standing will achieve this result in contemporary American culture. In addition, people might also be invited to participate bodily by raising their hands in the *orans* position, a gesture that I have seen work quite effectively in some churches. The renewal of the liturgy in the past twenty-five years has paid far too little attention to what one might call "the choreography of the assembly." Finally, the practice of a number of acclamations in the Eucharistic Prayers for Masses with Children ought to be adapted to all the Eucharistic Prayers. One thing that the survey reveals conclusively is that not only children have short attention spans.

## 2. Proclamation of the Word

The second major area that calls for reflection is the proclamation of the word. The balancing of more ritual factors with greater attention to the word of God has been one of the crowning achievements of the Second Vatican Council and of the subsequent liturgical reform.[26] The expansion of the Sunday, feast day, and daily Lectionaries has without a doubt enriched Catholics and inspired a profound desire among them for greater appreciation of the Scriptures. Yet the survey makes it quite clear that the proclamation of the word in the course of liturgical celebration is heard more for the quality and personality of the readers than for its content. In the interviews one finds the consistent comment that the lector read well, but the interviewee cannot really recall the content of the reading except perhaps for the biblical book it was taken from. (It would have been interesting to see how much of the Liturgy of the Word the interviewees recalled without prompting by the interviewers.)

All of this calls for some serious analysis. On the one hand, it must be admitted that the proclamation of the word is not a lecture class where students are expected to take notes and recall in detail the content of what was said. (Even the "less active" parishioners selected for the interviews seemed to me to be fairly involved in the church, and therefore one must surmise that the readings are not being heard at all by the vast majority of Catholic worshipers.) On the other hand, if a part of Scripture is proclaimed it should make some sort of impact. I suspect that, as was the case with the Eucharistic Prayer, the readings are not being heard because they are read ("proclaimed" would be too strong a word) without passion and conviction and without a great deal of interest. In an era when our attention is so clearly dominated by the electronic media, we need to recognize that the word of God will fall on deaf ears if it is not proclaimed with a sense that it is vital, indispensable for authentic human living. The first (but of course not only) criterion for lectors is that they believe what they are reading. This means not only that they read well but also that they have interiorized the meaning of what is to be proclaimed.

But the fault does not lie with the proclaimers alone. Without some form of introduction to the readings, listeners have no context to put them in. I for one am convinced that our liturgy needs less didacticism and not more, but it seems that some form of catechesis is called for here. This catechesis could be achieved in one of several ways. One approach would be to habituate parishioners in reading an introduction to the next week's Scriptures in the Sunday bulletin. Another would be to provide a brief oral introduction to the three readings either before the liturgy begins or just before the readings themselves.

A more radical solution would involve changing the time-honored sequence of the readings. Currently (and for as long as we have had descriptions of Christian worship) selections from the Bible are read in ascending order—from the least to the most important. There were a number of good reasons for doing this in the early Church. The typology and salvation-history view that Christians took made it logical to place the gospel at the culmination of the readings. Perhaps there was also an effort to differentiate the Christian biblical proclamation from that of the Jews, who read the Bible on the Sabbath in descending order—from the Law to the Prophets. The survey shows that if any of the readings "grabs" people, it is the gospel. Perhaps we ought to read the gospel first to provide some sort of context for the other readings. I cannot dwell here on the "problem" of the second reading. Except for the major seasons and feasts when all of the readings are interrelated, the second reading (from one of the New Testament letters) has no connection with either the selection from the Jewish Scriptures or the gospel. Despite the advantage of providing greater riches from the Bible, this reading is lost on most people; further reform of Catholic worship should consider dropping this second reading in the Sundays of the Year.

To summarize: Our theological statements about the nature and power of the Liturgy of the Word have not been matched by liturgical efforts or performance. Needless to say, the homily must also be included under this indictment, for it seems to me both on the basis of the survey and my observation that this is when worshipers are truly eager to hear something of significance for their lives. As Bishop Cummins, then chair of the Bishops' Committee on the Liturgy, remarked at the 1984 meeting of national liturgical commissions in Rome, homilizing "has often enough evidenced a mediocre practice."[27] In this area I would have to say there has been significant improvement in the twenty-five years of liturgical renewal. At least one could come to this conclusion on the basis of the majority of comments made in the survey. A cogent, coherent, succinct, and passionate homily that relates God's word to contemporary concerns remains, however, a great challenge to many preachers. I cannot even begin to analyze the reasons for this and possible solutions here. Suffice it to say that many preachers need to be convinced of the worthwhile nature of their task.

### 3. The Importance of Liturgy

The final area I have chosen for analysis is somewhat more intangible than either the Eucharistic Prayer or the Liturgy of the Word. Do people experience the Sunday liturgy as an important weekly event? On the basis of this survey and the similar study of American parishes undertaken by the University of Notre Dame,[28] it is difficult to express a simple judgment on this issue. Yet I believe it is one of the most important questions we need to ask.

The work of Vatican II and the subsequent efforts at renewal undertaken throughout the world point to the vital position that worship has in Christian life. One does not even need documents or theological analyses to come to the common-sense conclusion that the weekly assembly of Christians forms their identity as a people and provides the inspiration for their common mission. At the same time, it has been my frequent observation that many if not most worshiping assemblies do not sense the Sunday Eucharist as very important. Again, this is a quality that is not easy to pin down. It is analogous to Cardinal Newman's concept of "illative sense" in the arena of faith. That is to say, when all is said and done, an affirmation of faith involves not only rationally sound ideas but a sense of "thatness," an intuition of the inexplicable but nonetheless real truth of the object of belief, which demands commitment as well as intellectual agreement.

Why is this liturgical illative sense missing? The answer lies in vague and mysterious terms like "atmosphere" and "aura." It has everything to do with the nature of a liturgical space, the quality of its decorations, the lighting, acoustics, and, above all, the sense of excitement and engagement that animates the liturgical ministers. Such an illative sense is, as they say, caught rather than taught. The lack of it is what I think people are referring to when they claim that Catholic liturgy has lost its sense of mystery—a common enough complaint. This lament is so widespread that doubtless there is some truth to it. I fear, however, that what people mean by "mystery" has more to do with a "Wizard of Oz" image of liturgy and with a God whose transcendence is characterized by remoteness and wrath. The awe that the liturgical experience of the living God ought to inspire in us is not that of cringing serfs but of a people who pour out their profound gratitude for the mighty acts of God in Jesus Christ, who has set us free; it is the awe and reverence called for by the presence of God in the simplest and most human actions when they are performed in faith.

Merely to turn to past means for creating this sense is not a solution at all but an escape, an admission of defeat. No, the task of engendering an atmosphere in which the public liturgical activity of the Church not only is but seems important challenges us to be thoroughly contemporary while standing firmly in the tradition. And being contemporary does not mean surrendering to pop culture or the whim of the moment or to a superficial reaction to what people claim they are experiencing. It means being so thoroughly convinced that the ritual symbols of Christian faith are crucial for truly human life in this world that this conviction is contagious and apparent. This is what I mean by "the importance of liturgy."

### Conclusion

Needless to say, there are many other areas of the survey undertaken by the pastoral liturgical centers that could be examined here—the relationship of liturgy and music and the arts, further analysis of the corporate nature of Christian worship, the great change in the image and role of the priest. But as one of my favorite comments in the interviews stated (with regard to the length of the Sunday liturgy): "We can only endure so much." I have surveyed here only a few of the many important issues that surface in the survey—and these from the limited perspective of a liturgical theologian. I readily admit to some "waffling" as I studied the survey itself. At times it seemed to me that the liturgical renewal has proceeded apace and that the gains made by liturgical theology in the past century are well represented, at least in these fifteen parishes concerned with providing an excellent liturgy. At times I was struck by how many areas need vast improvement and by how little practice has kept pace with theory.

If this essay has for the most part concentrated on the latter set of reactions, it is most probably due to the personal predilections of the writer. Much remains to be accomplished, but much has already been accomplished. If this were not the case, celebrating the twenty-fifth anniversary of Vatican II's Constitution on the Sacred Liturgy would be neither appropriate nor fruitful. In my judgment we are well on the way toward the definitive reception of the council's work.

## Notes

1. See H. Kung, *Theology for the Third Millenium* (New York, 1988) 170–206. On the shift from classical to modern, see B. Lonergan, "Theology in its New Context," in B. Lonergan, *A Second Collection* (New York, 1975).

2. B. Leeming, *Principles of Sacramental Theology* (Westminster, Md., 1956).

3. B. Cooke, *Sacraments and Sacramentality* (Mystic, Conn., 1983).

4. R. Vaillancourt, *Toward a Renewal of Sacramental Theology* (Collegeville, 1979).

5. A. Kavanagh, *On Liturgical Theology* (New York, 1981); D. Power, *Unsearchable Riches: The Symbolic Nature of Liturgy* (New York, 1984); Robert Taft, chapters on the theology of the Liturgy of the Hours in his *Liturgy of the Hours in East and West* (Washington, 1986).

6. B. Lee, ed., 7 volumes (Collegeville, 1987).

7. K. Rahner, *The Church and the Sacraments*, ET (New York, 1963).

8. E. Schillebeeckx, *Christ: The Sacrament of the Encounter with God*, ET (New York, 1963).

9. See K. Rahner, "The Theology of the Symbol," *Theological Investigations* 4, ET (Baltimore, 1966) 221–252; on the symbolization process in general, see P. Berger, *The Sacred Canopy: Elements of a Sociological Theory of Religion* (New York, 1967); E. Cassirer, *An Essay on Man* (New Haven, 1944).

10. We have to be rather careful about our judgments of the theology of the past. While in many ways it may not be useful today, it emphasized values that we are apt to ignore. For an even-handed evaluation of models employed in various theologies of the liturgy, see J. Empereur, *Models of Liturgical Theology* (Alcuin/GROW Liturgical Study 4), Bramcote (Nottingham, 1987).

11. One exception is David Power, whose *Unsearchable Riches* is a valuable first attempt. Unfortunately Power's presuppositions are not laid out as clearly as one

might wish. Another tentative step in the development of such a critical hermeneutic is the work of Margaret Mary Kelleher, e.g. "Liturgical Theology: A Task and a Method," *Worship* 62 (1988) 2-25, based on the theological method of Bernard Lonergan.

12. Philadelphia, 1984.

13. For a critique of Eliade's approach somewhat akin to Lindbeck's point of view, see J. Z. Smith, *To Take Place: Toward Theory in Ritual* (Chicago, 1987), esp. 1-23; also the chapter entitled "The Wobbling Pivot" in his *Map Is Not Territory* (Leiden, 1978) 88-103.

14. Lindbeck, *Nature of Doctrine,* 17-18.

15. What I call here the "subjectivist bias" is treated as the "subjectification of reality" in a recent article by M. F. Mannion, "Liturgy and the Present Crisis of Culture," *Worship* 62 (1988), 102-107. For a similar cultural analysis of the social crisis facing liturgy, see R. T. Scott, "The Likelihood of Liturgy," *Anglican Theological Review* 62 (1980) 103-120.

16. See the perceptive comments on boredom and ritual in R. Taft, "Sunday in the Byzantine Tradition," in his *Beyond East and West: Problems in Liturgical Understanding* (Washington, 1984) 33, 43. As Taft says succinctly and quite correctly: "Variety is not the answer to trash."

17. Prosper of Aquitaine, *Indiculus de gratia Dei, Patrologia Latina* 51:209; see A. Kavanagh, *On Liturgical Theology* 3-22; see also P. DeClerck, "Lex Orandi, Lex Credendi: sens originel et avatars historiques d'un adage equivoque," *Questions Liturgiques* 59 (1978) 193-212.

18. M. F. Wiles, *The Making of Christian Doctrine* (London, 1967).

19. On this subject, see T. Berger, "Lex orandi, lex credendi, lex agendi: Auf dem Weg zu einer okumenisch konsensehaftigen Verhaltnisbestimmung von Liturgie, Theologie, und Ethik," *Archiv für Liturgiewissenschaft* 27 (1985) 425-432. This is also a concern of D. Power, *Unsearchable Riches.*

20. G. Lathrop, "Chronicle: AIDS and the Cup," *Worship* 62 (1988) 162-163.

21. See, for example, S. Langer, *Philosophy in a New Key,* 2nd ed. (Cambridge, Mass., 1978) 54-75; Power, *Unsearchable Riches,* 62-70. Several terms have been used for such multiple meaning in symbols. Power employs "polysemy" while I prefer "multivalence" or "polyvalence."

22. World Council of Churches, *Baptism, Eucharist, and Ministry* (Faith and Order Paper no. 111) (Geneva, 1982) "Eucharist," 3-26.

23. See further comment on this in my "Eucharist: Who May Preside?" *Commonweal* 115:15 (September 9, 1988) 462-466.

24. No. 54.

25. *To Give Thanks and Praise: General Instruction of the Roman Missal with Commentary for Musicians and Priests* (Washington, 1980) 139-151.

26. See, for example, The Constitution on the Sacred Liturgy, nos. 24, 35, 51; Introduction to the Lectionary, no. 10.

27. J. S. Cummins, "Twenty Years of Liturgical Renewal in the United States: Assessments and Prospects," in F. R. McManus, ed., *Thirty Years of Liturgical Renewal* (Washington: NCCB, 1987) 244.

28. See M. Searle, "The Notre Dame Study of Catholic Parish Life," *Worship* 60 (1986) 312-333.

# Liturgy and Social Concerns

*Peter J. Henriot, S.J.*

How do I come at this topic of liturgy and social concerns? What has been my experience? For eighteen of the twenty-five years since the promulgation of The Constitution on the Sacred Liturgy, I have celebrated each Sunday with parish communities in Seattle, Boston, Latin America, and Washington. Currently I help at St. Peter's on Capitol Hill and St. Aloysius, our Jesuit inner-city parish. And since 1971, I've been involved in the work of research, advocacy, and education on social issues at the Center of Concern. My challenge has been to link faith and justice. So I look forward to my task here this morning, drawing on my experience in both liturgy and social concerns.

My task this Sunday morning is to raise points that I have heard since Friday afternoon, points that come to me in particular from the perspective of social concerns. I want to explore three themes:

1. Links between liturgy and social concerns;
2. Issues and values that raise questions for me/us;
3. Actions that need to be taken as follow-up.

## Links

My thesis is very simple. There is an integral link between liturgy and life, between the celebration of liturgy and the doing of justice, between public worship and political action, in the sense of building the city of humans, as Monika Hellwig stressed (see p. 60ff.).

This thesis is *empirically* verified in the history of the liturgical movement. At least in this country, the persons who were influential early in the liturgical movement were also deeply involved in the social movement. This was brought home to me just seven years ago this

week, on the occasion of the funeral of Dorothy Day. I was privileged
to take the great Jesuit apostle for Washington's poor, Fr. Horace
McKenna, S.J., up to New York for his friend Dorothy's funeral. As
we sat in the back row of that crowded church in the Bowery, I was
surprised when Godfrey Diekmann turned to greet us. Surprised because I had thought he was dead! And surprised because I didn't know
of his connection with Dorothy Day and the Catholic Worker movement. Later I learned that Peter Maurin, cofounder with Dorothy of
the Catholic Worker, was close to Virgil Michel and used to spend time
at St. John's in Collegeville. In Virgil Michel, of course, liturgical renewal was accompanied by interest in many social issues. His writings and actions showed this. The National Liturgical Weeks used to
attract a very broad spectrum of the Church and always included topics
of social concern on the agenda.

The link between liturgy and social concerns also is *theologically*
verified. As we have been reminded here several times during this colloquium, the Greek meaning of the word "liturgy" is "public service,"
"work undertaken on behalf of people," "work of the people." Liturgy is the faith work, the celebration of the people of whom *Gaudium
et spes* (Pastoral Constitution on the Church in the Modern World of
the Second Vatican Council) says: "The joys and hopes, the sorrows
and anxieties of the women and men of this age, especially the poor
and those in any way oppressed, these are the joys and hopes, the
sorrows and anxieties, of the followers of Jesus." The U.S. bishops'
economic pastoral states: "No one can claim the name Christian who
is comfortable in the face of the hunger, the homelessness, the injustice
and oppression in this country and around the world."

This theological link is found in the Eucharist. It is there that the
offering and sharing of bread occurs—the elemental sign of justice in
community, the basic necessity of survival in dignity. For this reason,
we have what Don Saliers referred to as the "eschatological dimension" of all liturgical acts (see p. 76, 80ff.): the bringing together of
Church, world, and reign.

It seems imperative to me, therefore, that the *effective* dimension
of liturgy be examined carefully, not just the *performative-celebrative*
dimension. This is the question about the liturgy raised by William
McCready: "What difference does it make in the life of the parish?"[1]
And the question of John Baldovin: "What kind of (moral) activity is
characteristic of people of faith, people who have been formed by liturgical worship?" (see p. 103).

*Issues and Values*

The link between liturgy and social concerns, therefore, has raised several issues and values, which come to me from my two days of listening and participating here. Let me briefly mention six of them, in ways that can only be suggestive.

1. There is a disturbing absence of attention in this colloquium to the link between liturgy and social concerns. It is a key question to be studied in any thorough examination of parishes, yet it is inadequately represented in the assessment of liturgical renewal, done in fifteen places across the country. The question was not explicitly asked in the interview instrument, nor was it explicitly reflected on in the eight major presentations.

How central is this link to the life and practice of the liturgical centers that are cosponsoring this colloquium? I believe it is important to recall Aidan Kavanagh's comment that social concern and liturgical renewal were movements fertilized together and that separation leads to disaster on both sides.

2. Community has been an important consideration here, with much discussion of what makes a functional community—size, character, and the like. But the challenge is to make worshiping communities diverse, reflective of what Roger Haight referred to as "graced assemblies of existential variation" (see p. 32). This means diversity of ethnic background, class, and so on.

There is certainly a danger in some parish settings of what has been called here "embourgeoisment" or "middle classification" of liturgical life. Gerard Sloyan reminded us of Paul's strictures in I Corinthians 11 about the social harmony that should prevail in a liturgical celebration (see p. 47). If wider needs are not being attended to, the Eucharist is not valid, no matter how "renewed" it may be.

This is a challenge to the U.S. Church regarding inclusion of blacks, Hispanics, Asians, and other minorities. It is a challenge to this very gathering here. How can we broaden the "existential variation" of our assemblies?

3. Monika Hellwig in her presentation spoke of the modeling of values that goes on in the celebration of liturgies and of the implicit theologies manifested. According to the U.S. Bishops' economic pastoral, the value of participation is central to a just social life. The participation of all is an important social goal. Hence the question of "ownership" of the liturgy, raised so strongly by William McCready,

is more than simply a matter of the effectiveness of the liturgical renewal. It is a matter of its justice. It is in this light, I believe, that we need to consider the issues Ronald Grimes pointed to concerning the "politics of planning" and the effects of "democratization" (see p. 18).

In evaluating liturgical renewal, then, we need to ask, How just is the celebration in itself?

4. That brings me to the issue of women as an explicit justice issue in liturgical celebration. Frankly, it has been very surprising to me as a celebrant active in parish life that this issue was not reflected on more widely in the various presentations we have heard during the past two days. I feel, from my own experience, that the issue of women and liturgy is much more alive and central than this colloquium has so far acknowledged.

There is the issue of inclusive language—such a small point with such large implications! Pronouns *are* substance. And it takes very little effort by intelligent and good-willed people to use inclusive language. Granted, there are deeper theological points to be dealt with about the nature of the Godhead. It may take longer to settle that than it does to determine whether we use "sisters and brothers" in our greetings. Let's do what we can do now, and do it joyfully!

The issue of the ordination of women, of course, won't go away—and it is only heightened by the silliness surrounding the "altar girl" controversy. (At St. Peter's, we have solved that very minor problem—we only have "altar creatures," and they come in a variety of sizes, colors, and sexes!) It seems to me that a breakthrough in the question of ordination may come when we honestly ask why the *ritual*—celebration—is tied to the *jurisdictional*—power, and why this linkage is allowed to prevent thousands of parishes and millions of people from having regular Eucharistic liturgies. (Similar questions must be asked, of course, in connection with the mandatory celibacy law.)

In addressing the issue of women and liturgy, it seems to me that the next steps are up to men in the Church; they must be more assertive in seeking justice. And I say that as a male Jesuit cleric who enjoys considerable privilege. How willing are we men to work for justice in liturgies?

5. The issue of teaching arises in the celebration of the liturgy. What is the didactic or prophetic character of liturgy as regards social concerns? Yes, we need to model values of peace and justice. But is there something more that we need to do? To be honest, today the basic,

most widely accessible place for teaching in the Church is the Sunday morning parish liturgy, not the declining school system and certainly not adult discussion groups. Where will the peace pastoral and the economic pastoral be explained if not in the course of the liturgy?

This has implications for many elements in the liturgy, not the least of which is the homily. I believe that Monika Hellwig put this point very well in her usual perceptive fashion when she said, "We don't come to liturgy simply to pray but to listen, not simply to renew our commitment but to learn more about what that commitment means" (see p. 62ff.). The challenge is, How do our liturgies teach social concerns to the people?

6. I mention enculturation as the last issue, and I recognize that it may be the most significant challenge of the next twenty-five years of liturgical renewal—here in the United States as well as in the Third World. Many of the presentations mentioned this issue, and it is a key social concern. In this country we face the issue of making liturgies true celebrations of the experiences of blacks, Hispanics, Asians, the poor, women, gays, etc. The role of experience is, of course, very important. I thought of that when I heard reference made several times to the practice of holding hands during the Our Father. Does the experience of this as a good thing in some places—St. Aloysius here in D.C., for instance—have a bearing on what is or is not authentic enculturation?

How do we go about authentic enculturation without succumbing to dangerous acculturation—that is, simply adapting to and adopting the dominant culture and losing the unique gospel contribution?

### Actions

Let me briefly conclude with some suggestions for actions that are appropriate to this focus on the link between liturgy and social concerns. As part of the follow-up to this colloquium, we all need to ask ourselves how in our personal lives we can better link social concerns and liturgy. As participants, planners, teachers, celebrants, what can we personally do? Then, in our corporate lives, we need to ask this same question. In our various centers, in meetings such as this, how do we make explicit this linkage?

Regarding the future, I would certainly recommend more study be done of the effective character of liturgical renewal, that is, study of what is happening in the mission of the Church as a result of liturgical celebrations. In the parishes studied in this project and in other studies, we should find out what difference liturgical celebrations make in the lives of people in terms of their commitment to being followers of Jesus, sensitive to the "joys and hopes, sorrows and anxieties of all women and men, especially the poor and oppressed."

I believe that there should be more cooperation between liturgists and social-action people. I was pleased to learn that in the North American Academy of Liturgy there is a worship and social justice section. Given the strong emphasis of the U.S. bishops in their pastoral letters on peace and on economic justice, this section should be a lively one.

### Conclusion

Godfrey Diekmann summed up for me this link between the liturgy and social concerns by reflecting on the link that existed in the life of Virgil Michel. He noted that Virgil's own personal interest centered largely in social justice and quotes the appraisal of Fr. H. R. Reinhold regarding the connection of social justice with a new social spirituality: "For Fr. Virgil Michel the labor encyclicals of Leo XIII and the liturgical reforms of Pius X did not just by accident happen within one generation, but were responses to cries of the masses for Christ, who had power and gave the good tidings. They belonged together."[2]

My sisters and brothers, today they still belong together, social concerns and liturgical renewal. And that should keep us all busy for the next twenty-five years!

### Notes

1. William McCready's presentation is not included in this volume.
2. "Presentation of the Berakah Award," *Worship* 51:4 (July 1977) 363.

# Reflections from the Hispanic Viewpoint

*Juan J. Sosa*

In just a few months the Instituto de Liturgia Hispana will celebrate its tenth anniversary. From the heavily populated cities of the Northeast to the rapidly growing centers of the Southwest, from Los Angeles to Portland and Yakima, from San Antonio to Chicago, throughout these ten years the leadership of the Instituto has traveled to meet with and share ideas with Hispanic Catholics. They have done this for two principal reasons: (1) to help the bishops of the United States carry out the reforms of Vatican II and (2) to develop liturgical enculturation among Hispanic communities.

At first the enterprise was difficult and, for some, discouraging. The overall experience, however, has turned out to be quite the opposite. The Instituto has uncovered encouraging facts in the different communities visited:

- not different languages, but different accents;
- not different and clashing melodies, but different rhythms;
- not different images of Christ, but a composite icon of a liberating servant;
- not different visions of Church, but different expressions of the same post–Vatican II vision: a pilgrim people at prayer who long to experience liberation through fiesta, contemplation, movement, and silence.

The journey of the Instituto leadership throughout its short history is by no means unique. Before the Instituto was formed, many dedicated leaders had embarked upon a similar journey, wandering through the crowded streets of urban centers in the Northeast or through quiet desert communities in the Southwest. They had listened to and worked with Hispanic Catholics in our country in ways that deserve commendation and praise.

The uniqueness of the Instituto's journey lies in its focus. These Hispanic liturgists have not focused on ideological issues or political positions in their efforts to promote liturgical formation and enculturation. Rather, they have focused on the need to explicate the mystery of God in the lives of people who have been undergoing enormous social change with grave consequences to their value systems. In simple terms, the Instituto's journey focused on the need and desire to help Hispanic people pray at their best.

Allow me to share with you, briefly, the key issues that have dominated our efforts:

### Integration

While the issue of enculturation is of obvious importance, it is linked with another equally important issue that affects any cultural group developing in the United States, namely, integration. If cultural pluralism is to emerge as a viable option in our country, integration, as the process whereby cultural groups meet and form a mosaic of cultural traits and attitudes in society, must work.

We owe a debt of gratitude to anthropologists such as Herskovitz and Fernando Ortiz who have shed light on the reciprocal nature of the process of cultural integration, but one need not forget that the process of integration became the trademark of the Master himself, for whom a Roman centurion, a Jewish fisherman, or a Samaritan pilgrim were as important as the Jewish liturgists of his time. Indeed, cultural pluralism as the basis and integration as the process became the trademarks of the earliest communities of the Church. In the best catholic tradition of our Church, Hispanic Catholics today long to experience integration as a reciprocal and dynamic process through which groups of people in our society can be different and yet become one.

There are three essential ingredients in this process:

1. *Diversity.* Diversity is not a threat. It is all right to be different because we are enriched by those who are different from us. Can it be possible that some of the problems our speakers found in the fifteen parishes studied had to do with a lack of diversity? Some people claim that if violence begets violence, sameness probably begets dullness.

2. *Selectivity.* There is a need to be selective in the cultural traits one group borrows from another. It is all right to exchange cultural

traits so long as the transaction does not threaten the group's value system. There is a process involved here whereby people move from an awareness of tangible practices to intangible values. Could it be possible that the aggressive behavior of some Hispanic groups stems from a lack of understanding about this process?

3. *Contact with our roots.* It is good to experience from time to time a celebration by which I can experience my Hispanic roots. This enables me to move toward integration with the larger community with comfort. My cultural batteries need to be recharged from time to time.

Hispanic Catholics have a rich mythology in their tradition and multifaceted rituals connected with that mythology. Here they discover a wealth of resources that help them pray and live at their best. We need to recognize the need for Hispanic Catholics to stay in contact with their roots so that they can feel more at home as they engage in the process of integration.

*Enculturation*

Staying in touch with our roots is an obvious necessity when dealing with the question of enculturation. But I hope we have moved beyond making superficial changes such as those we refer to as the serape syndrome. The syndrome is in evidence when someone throws a colorful serape on the altar or drapes one around the presider's neck and presumes the liturgy is "enculturated." We need to look deeper and discover the intangible values and their related tangible forms that are involved. We will discover a rich mythological world that can develop and shape those who come in contact with it.

Allow me to conclude with four summary statements and questions that might help us reflect on Hispanic concerns:

1. Although we can follow guidelines on multilingual masses and achieve a certain amount of success in bilingual and trilingual celebrations, can we speak of languages at worship if the communities involved are not engaged in a reciprocal process of accepting and respecting each other, that is, if cultural *pluralism* does not permeate their tasks and projects?

2. Whereas we must continue to explore the issue of liturgical enculturation among Hispanic Catholics, can we ever deal with this issue adequately without facing the challenges of *integration*?

3. Whereas Hispanic communities are enriched by a tradition of five hundred years, containing a multiplicity of symbols and rituals,

should we speak of new symbols before we fully understand which symbols and rituals recharge the batteries of our Hispanic communities in traditional celebrations?

4. "Folk piety" and "popular religion" have been designated as approaches for evangelistic efforts among Hispanics and non-Hispanics. But can we accept that Mary and the saints are the embodiment of Scripture for Hispanics, the models of a true and final liberation toward which we all must strive?

Perhaps the time has come to attempt to measure not the surface components of the reform but the actual object of the reform, the *renewal of our hearts* and the hearts of our communities, which dare mirror the many features of a suffering and liberating Christ.

# Speaking in the Future Tense

## Kathleen Hughes, R.S.C.J.

**I** am delighted and honored to be a participant in this colloquium. I want to congratulate the directors and staffs of the four liturgical centers for the long and careful preparations, the amassing of so much raw data, and the selection of interpreters, each of whom, in these last two days, has helped us analyze and assess the material assembled, product of twenty-five years of liturgical renewal. As we raise a toast today on this anniversary of the promulgation of The Constitution on the Sacred Liturgy, we turn ahead to consider the next twenty-five years.

Shortly after I was asked to conclude this colloquium by suggesting some of the future directions for liturgical renewal in the American Church, I was told the following story:

There is a French-speaking couple at the University of Notre Dame who invited a visiting professor from France to their home—and they rounded out the guest list with one of the Notre Dame administrators. Now this last named was an *English*-speaking woman, but she said to herself: "We'll probably be speaking in French, but I can handle it! I may not be fluent, but I can certainly manage to keep up a conversation." In fact, as dinner progressed she thought she was communicating quite nicely until the visiting professor pushed his chair away from the table and exclaimed: "I must go home. This woman is incapable of speaking in the future tense."

We are assembled at the conclusion of this colloquium to speak in the future tense.

It is a *particular* challenge to be the last speaker. After reading all the data assembled by and about fifteen worshiping communities and all of the papers of the other speakers, I paced around a lot. I am not—I

125

suspect none of us is—dispassionate about the liturgy, else we wouldn't
be committing our lives to the academic or the pastoral work of liturgical renewal. Besides being believers, we have our own professional
preoccupations, prejudices, and investments. Occasionally I found myself challenged by the data, occasionally surprised, and once or twice
mystified. However, my strongest *initial* response was to want to distance myself from some of these parishes, alternately amused or annoyed by what I was reading, but intent to convey to *you* that X custom
or Y interpretation was certainly not what my colleagues and I are
teaching at the Catholic Theological Union!

Then an interesting question occurred to me: Would the Eucharist
we would celebrate together during this conference be appreciably
different than that of our fifteen parishes if submitted to the same study
instrument? Think about it. I have a suspicion that we would bring
a variety of different and sometimes conflicting criteria to bear on our
assessments; that we would probably be sensitive to totally different
elements; that we may have been more attentive to *how* things were
done and *who* did them than to *what* was done; and we may well have
found ourselves occasionally inattentive to the ritual as were our interviewees, perhaps even during the readings or the Eucharistic Prayer.
What would we make of our own experience at worship? What would
others make of it? How would it look on paper?

The wisdom of one respondent is apposite. I refer to the person
who urged reeducation for everyone over thirty and then concluded
with this admission: "Reeducation is what it takes for [the Eucharist]
to be really prayer. . . . For a whole bunch of people, sure it's prayer.
But I have a feeling that there are some people for whom it's not. And
those are the ones I worry about. And sometimes, you know, that's
me."[1] Is Pogo right? Is it possible that we have met the enemy and
they are us?

With a newfound humility I returned to the data. I decided not
to highlight all of those practices where you and I know better. This
would only produce a list of abuses for our correction over the next
twenty-five years, a wearisome project indeed. Rather, I will examine
the data, in dialogue with the remarks of my colleagues, for signs of
hope, for I believe our future agenda must be constructed on the bedrock of our present strength. Accordingly, what follows are remarks
in two parts. First, as the First Epistle of Peter urges, I "will give an
account of the hope that is in me" (1 Pet 3:15), and second, I will suggest an agenda for the future, once we are rooted in confident hope.

## Giving an Account of the Hope That Is in Me

What I propose to do is to sketch a composite picture of the preparation and celebration of a Sunday liturgy according to *Liturgical Renewal: 1963–1988,* and in the process to identify signs of hope and promise.

### Preparation

First, liturgical preparation—what used to be called "liturgy planning" until Austin Fleming set us straight.[2] Preparation is essential because of the variety of events that find their way into the Sunday celebration. In the fifteen parishes that were visited, communities celebrated a golden wedding anniversary, five baptisms, a single baptism, the entry into the catechumenate, Teaching Sunday, Toy Sunday, and the feast of Christ the King—which happened to be the titular feast of that parish. What ever happened to "ordinary time"? In addition, a number of these communities have a separate Liturgy of the Word for children, which obviously demands further attention and preparation. The words of one participant ring true: "Nothing is ever normal; we must always adapt."

Regarding preparation, I would not be so sanguine as one of the participants, who said, "Even at our worst, we're competent!" but I do find cause for hope in another's assessment: "We feel very free and able to be creative in preparing what the Church already gives us without 'scrambling' to find new American gimmicks." Those who prepare liturgy give evidence of a developing facility to choose among options as appropriate to feast or season, for example, the sprinkling rite, the gospel procession, the use of incense, the variety of penitential options, a thoughtful selection of the Eucharistic Prayer, a wider repertoire and more sensitive selection of music, and so on.

Some communities make more radical structural adaptations of the rite, occasionally demonstrating a certain overenthusiasm for pruning, but, by and large, acting responsibly in the void of officially sponsored experimentation.

Enthusiasm for "theme Mass planning" has clearly declined—and that's cause for *great* hope. When the word "theme" was applied to the liturgy by one respondent, the "theme" was not an idea invented and superimposed on the celebration but derived specifically from the readings of the day as well as from the presidential prayers and the preface.

Parenthetically, our liturgy "preparers" demonstrate remarkable facility with a new liturgical terminology, and it appears to coexist peacefully with an older vocabulary. "Transubstantiation" slid easily off one tongue, but so did "catechumen" off another, and "mystagogy," "preparation rites," "RCIA," "Form C" (identified quite correctly as a litany of praise), "homily," "liturgy," "confirmandi," "responsorial psalm," "immersion pools," "acclamations," even "scrutinies"—though one could almost see the woman shudder who declared this "a dreadful name."

There is a complex relationship between language and consciousness that cannot be developed here. Suffice it to say that language encodes and shapes reality within a particular discourse situation. The very use of this post–Vatican II terminology is shaping the community's sacramental consciousness in new ways.

## Many Ministries

The phenomenon of burgeoning liturgical ministries is evident in the study. I accept Monika Hellwig's caution that we could be witnessing the development of a new paraclergy, "self-selected liturgical ministers saving the rest of us the trouble of active involvement" (see p. 57). The *Notre Dame Study of Catholic Parish Life*[3] had raised a similar concern about the possibility of a new clerical caste made up of those with degrees in liturgy and/or religious education. It is something to guard against!

Yet among our respondents I cannnot detect an attitude of elitism, but rather mutuality, collaboration, and inclusion. Two thoughtful responses support this contention, the first: "I guess there will always be those of us who are standing much closer to the center of the whole operation with great eagerness that everybody move in and see what we see"; and the second: "[When] I've helped plan or . . . I have an active role, I'm more and more concerned about [what the average Joe is experiencing] because I think sometimes I have a false sense of what it is."

I suppose "ministry" is an abused word. It could well be evacuated of all meaning if it becomes too porous. Yet I believe there is justification for speaking legitimately about the ministry of the whole assembly. To speak of the ministry of the assembly is to speak of active participation in its conscious, sacramental dimensions—the goal of the liturgical movement, but a goal that seems to elude us even to this day. Nevertheless, I find the numbers engaged in liturgical ministry to be truly astounding—and I name as cause for hope that the gifts of many are being placed at the service of the assembly, that these people are being trained and rehearsed and, at a deeper level, offered days of retreat and reflection for the development of their own ministerial identity.

*Introductory Rites*

I turn now to the gathering rites and the celebration itself. One person described the act of assembling with this image: "It's the people humanizing the building and the building giving grandeur and dignity to the people." That insight is simply another way of expressing the theology of grace, which led Roger Haight to speak of the people "bringing grace as they gather" (see p. 30).

Fair enough! But what of socializing before the Eucharist? Does grace have to be boisterous and noisy? Is this a good custom or not? The communities of our study described themselves as warm and welcoming, making persons feel comfortable. Some regarded these moments of socializing as high points of the celebration, whether they occurred at the beginning or end. I must join my colleagues in expressing concern, not so much that socializing takes place before Mass but that greeting one another warmly seems to be identified as a "high point" rather than the word of God, the Eucharistic Prayer, or the reception of Communion. (But we would not be honest if we did not also acknowledge that "socializing" was a focus of one of the questions in the study, and people tended to talk most about what they were asked about. Perhaps, in this case, we led the witnesses!)

That being said, the gathering and welcoming may well be a cause for hope! Several communities were particularly sensitive to welcoming the strangers, the visitors, the inquirers, the disaffected, the disenfranchised. They hoped their liturgy would be inclusive in instances when some arrived who were alienated. Surely these concerns go beyond the desire for a cozy sense of belonging and togetherness and give evidence of outreach and mission rooted in an express ecclesiology. As articulated by one respondent: "We are the face of the Church, especially for new people."

For our participants, the welcoming rites seem to constitute part of the celebration, not an appendage. We might simply note in passing that social interaction followed by music rehearsals and a commentator's introduction have placed an even greater strain on what Ralph Keifer once called "our cluttered vestibule" of entrance rites.[4] I am grateful to William McCready for the insight that maybe what we see here is typical of Americans, namely, that we tend to fill up on appetizers and then have no room for the nourishing meal that follows.[5]

## Liturgy of the Word

There is cause for hope in what appears to be a real hunger for Scripture in the communities surveyed. Each community reports that the word proclaimed is from the *Lectionary*. This is the more remarkable in parishes where there seems to be a significant amount of improvisation of presidential prayers, the substitution of the Italian Sacramentary, and, in one case, the bald admission that "the presider does not use the *Sacramentary*." Furthermore, with the exception of services for children, all three readings are proclaimed and a responsorial psalm is also used.

With regard to the homily, I question Dr. McCready's assertion that preaching is less good than it was some years ago. It is my suspicion that the quality of preaching may have changed less than we think. What have changed are people's expectations and demands—and that, I think, is another cause for hope.

A good homily "comes out of the readings and not the homilist's agenda," said one, and this sentiment was frequently echoed in concern that the homily be related to the word of God, give a better understanding of the gospel, challenge the community "to look beyond, or move beyond, or think beyond, or not be stagnant," have a "build the kingdom here" idea, and, finally, serve as a type of fulcrum, moving the community to the Eucharistic table. One person stated emphatically that "a good homily will last ten minutes and make three points"—this from someone obviously under the spell of Father Walter Burghardt!

It is an interesting phenomenon that the ministry of preaching has been opened up to the laity among communities of our study. The conviction was expressed that "ordained or unordained, all have a life of faith." Homilies are given by missionaries, seminarians, ministers of other denominations, and members of the pastoral staff, both women and men. But not just anyone is welcomed to preach the word of God. The community expects that its homilist will (1) have an active life of faith, (2) have a pastoral relationship with the community, and (3) have appropriate training for the ministry. In my judgment that is a very wise set of criteria. Parenthetically, the development of a pastoral relationship prior to liturgical ministry is also expected of a presider. One community was particularly emphatic about the havoc caused by "visiting priests."

People know what they want of a homily and why. "A good homily," said one, "will linger in the head for days and days." And another recognized the phenomenon that "a day or two later, for some reason the reading may hit. . . . It's like delayed reaction," an explosion of the Spirit. Perhaps we need be less concerned that people could not remember specific parts of the celebration in the recall interviews, which took place immediately after the celebration, and recognize the gradual and almost imperceptible ways that the word and the rite work their way into our very being. It takes time.

The general intercessions seem to be very well prepared and the range of community concerns is appropriately broad. Spontaneous prayer, however, met with mixed review. Said one realist: "Some people know how to pray and others don't." Praying, it would seem, is a little like being able—or not able—to tell a joke. For that reason, prayers of intercession prepared in advance of the celebration are cause for hope.

## The Liturgy of the Eucharist

With regard to the Eucharistic Prayer, it is clear that this appears to be the dullest part of the celebration for some, as John Baldovin mentioned in his talk yesterday. As one person observed, "It [the Eucharistic Prayer] is easily ignored." On the other hand, another respondent, who quickly passed over the Eucharistic Prayer to speak about the Our Father and the exchange of peace, simply noted of the Eucharistic Prayer: "It's the basics." This led me to wonder what's really happening.

I'd like to propose to you my Egeria theory. Egeria was a fourth-century nun who made a pilgrimage from Spain to the Holy Land. During her travels she kept a diary addressed to the Mothers and Sisters back home, recording her adventures, mostly of the liturgical variety.[5] What she records is not what her friends back home already know. Rather, she records what she finds particularly interesting and unusual. Is it possible that our participants skip over the Eucharistic Prayer in their narration of the celebration because "it's the basics" rather than an innovation of Vatican II? This is just one of numerous hypotheses I would love to be able to test when Ronald Grimes helps us redesign our survey instrument for long-term field research.

There is another phenomenon with regard to Eucharistic Prayers that I find fascinating in this study, namely, that those who do speak about them acknowledge that they pray them inwardly along with the presider: "It's a silent time," said one, "but people have the words in their hearts and minds and can pray along with him." And another added: "I'm listening, I'm participating, and half the time I'm saying it. You tend to memorize some of these things, having heard it so many times." Yet another spoke about the familiarity of the words as playing an important role in inviting the community's prayer and then stated emphatically: "The Eucharistic Prayer is *not* the presider's private devotion."

What is it then? As Gerard Sloyan noted, most Catholics may have difficulty articulating their faith (see p. 48)—but not the following respondent: "[In the Eucharistic Prayer] we are praying that the purpose for which we are gathered, the celebration of this Eucharist, that it all be fit and acceptable to God the Father; that the offering that we have prepared will be for us that which we desire, a means of sharing that body and blood of Christ of which we are a part, that God will make the offerings the body and blood of Christ that we are here to share." To this, another added: "I always had this idea that the priest is up there . . . and there's this incredible thing that happens: The bread and wine become [Christ's] body and blood. And then all of a sudden I realized it's us too, the community as well." This person did not explicitly mention the Spirit of God, but surely here the transforming action of God's Spirit is implicitly named and acknowledged.

I find cause for hope—indeed, for rejoicing—that active participation includes this kind of participation in the Eucharistic Prayer and that it has led at least some among us to a deeper faith and its articulation.

Holding hands at the Our Father and the extended exchange of Christ's peace have received ample mention by others. I will pass on to the reception of Communion, only pausing long enough to ponder what's it like in the community that reported, "Occasionally we all sing the Our Father together, like Perry Como."

*Communion*

There is no more remarkable phenomenon of our renewed rites than the nearly complete participation of the assembly in Communion. One parish said its participation was about 85 percent, but most were in the 90 percent–95 percent range, and one community said 99 percent of the community were communicants. Receiving Communion, like anything else, can become routine, of course. But there are flashes of insight among the respondents, such as the communicant who said: "I'm conscious of what I'm doing. It scares the heck out of me sometimes."

Besides this increase in the numbers who receive Communion, there is a shift in the way the Communion and post-Communion periods are experienced. Not so long ago, the post-Communion period was the most private moment for solitary prayer. Now, for many respondents in the survey, this is a time to recognize themselves as part of the whole Christ. Several in the survey report that after receiving Communion they deliberately watch the faces of others in the Communion procession. Said one: "I feel a communion with everyone else. I try to feel myself a part of a bigger community rather than just turning inward."

Perhaps it is to this larger vision and commitment that another respondent alluded: "I'm learning more and more what it means to be the Body of Christ. . . . It is very difficult for me not to show up on a given Sunday for liturgy." Sounds like a latter-day echo of the Martyrs of Abysinia who, when asked why they continued to celebrate the Eucharist after being forbidden to do so, responded, "We could not live without it." Or, in the patois of our own study: "If we don't, we aren't. It is something we cannot not do." That profound commitment to Eucharist is surely cause for hope.

### Future Agenda

Twenty-five years of liturgical renewal, and yet in many ways we have only just begun. There is a wonderful passage in Annie Dillard's book *Teaching a Stone to Talk* in which she puzzles over the liturgical reforms of Vatican II: "Who gave these nice Catholics guitars?" she asks. "Why are they not mumbling in Latin and performing superstitious rituals? What is the Pope thinking of?"[6]

That's a tricky question! In lieu of his answer, I will suggest some items that I believe must now find a place on our agenda. Many of these issues have crystallized during our days together. All of them, in my judgment, are predicated on serious collaboration between scholars and practitioners of the kind that has been so fruitful during these days.

Consider for a moment who will gather to celebrate the fiftieth anniversary of The Constitution on the Sacred Liturgy. We have to be aware, as we "speak in the future tense," that the Roman Catholic Church in the United States is undergoing dramatic changes, radical changes: in its multicultural composition, in those who choose to be professional ministers within its ranks, in a new feminist consciousness that barely surfaced in the fifteen parishes of our study, in a distancing from the concerns of the Church of Rome on the part of some and a militancy to uphold the tottering edifice of Rome on the part of others. More and more, since we are growing in our appreciation that *we* are the Church, these issues are going to be played out within rather than outside the walls of our assemblies. So be it.

(The agenda that follows is arranged according to the order in which these issues surfaced in the first half of my paper.)

A first agenda item: *The question of Ordinary Time.* Why, Sunday after Sunday, do we add other events to our celebration of word and sacrament? Ronald Grimes suggested to me that the communities of the study "got dressed up for their visit just as we might dress up for a photograph." While that may explain why so many of the parishes "got dressed up"; nevertheless, it is happening with increasing frequency that wedding anniversaries, engagements, infant baptisms, anointings, and so on, are finding their way into Sunday parish celebrations.

Now the problem is that additional rites place an enormous burden on those who prepare and an equally difficult burden on the homilist because these celebrations take place after the Liturgy of the Word. The homily is rooted in the Scriptures of the day and directed to the community who have gathered for Eucharist, but the homilist cannot ignore a third point of reference, namely, the anniversary or baptism or whatever additional rite is being celebrated. It is my suspicion that the power of the word is being diffused because of some of these events. I don't suggest that we shouldn't have celebrations such as the entrance into the catechumenate on a Sunday, but I do suggest that we must be cautious about the frequency with which other events obscure the clarity and simplicity of word and table and diffuse the power of the word of God.

*The homily* itself is a major concern in the survey. There is, on the one hand, a strongly stated hunger for the word of God. There is, on the other hand, a nearly universal dissatisfaction with the current level of preaching. It *must* improve. That means there has to be enormous energy and time spent, not simply on people who are in seminaries—though that's not a bad place to begin—but even more urgently in the area of continuing education of the clergy. Furthermore, it is clear from the parishes studied that the gift for preaching has been identified in others besides the ordained. Discovery and development of the preaching charism is critical in our day. Surely, however, all preaching, not just that of the ordained, belongs after the proclamation of the word of God, not after the introductory greeting or the prayer after Communion.[7]

*The Eucharistic Prayer*—and people's conscious participation in it—was another concern of the study. While many respondents passed over this prayer in silence, perhaps more interested in reporting what they perceived as "the highlights," other respondents reported praying the Eucharistic Prayer along with the presider. This prayer, it appears, functions as a type of mantra, a form of prayer which one does not necessarily remember afterward word for word but which works its way into the heart and flesh. I think we do not need to elaborate long on this. What I do believe is needed is for presiders to pray it as if they mean it. In the worship practicum class at Catholic Theological Union, I urge my students in the course of the quarter in which they are learning to preside to take the texts of the Eucharistic Prayers for their solitary prayer times, day after day. In this way they learn the prayers "by heart." In this way they will sound as if they mean them when they preside.

*Ritual pruning.* This is the issue of structural changes that have or should take place in the Roman rite. In the communities of our survey, some simply omitted parts of the rite on occasion, such as the *Gloria* or the Creed; others made more radical adaptations: dropping the prayer over the gifts or the preface dialogue or, in one case, even the preface. What is happening, I think, is akin to what John Baldovin suggested yesterday: We have an exceptionally wordy liturgy. Because there is no officially sponsored experimentation, people are adapting the rite at will, for good reasons or for ill.

One problem, among others, that the International Commission on English in the Liturgy faces as it tries to prepare the revised edition of the *Roman Missal* is that it has no authority to make any structural adaptations in the Roman Rite unless mandated by a conference of bishops. Diocesan and national liturgical offices have to be informed of what is actually happening in local communities and need to assist in careful evaluation of such experimentation. Only in this way will appropriate recommendations be formulated for the work of revision of the *Roman Missal*.

*Symbolic Perception* was a category that received much attention during the last two days, particularly the loss of primary symbols. The power of the symbols of word and table seems to have receded, its place usurped by greetings, handholding, and the like. One person lamented, ''The Eucharist is squished between music.'' This may well be a problem that must be addressed in preparing celebrations.

Liturgical preparation is not a linear but a spiral process. The first question is not What shall we sing for the entrance procession? The first question is, What is the heart of the celebration? How can we lift up and highlight today's word and sacrament? Then, being of the minimalist school, I would urge that preparing be very cautious, judicious, and simple so that we don't have one long undifferentiated experience—nothing highlighted because everything is deemed of equal importance.

Aidan Kavanagh, following Josef Jungmann, praised ''pious conservation'' alongside adaptation (see p. 90). In preparing liturgy, pious conservation invites retrieval of the noble simplicity of the Roman Rite. In my judgment, preparing or planning liturgy *can* be done by committee. In fact, it *must* be done by a committee, since the alternative appears to be that preparing belongs to the presider alone, a position not supported by the General Instruction of the Roman Missal, which calls for collaboration.[8] The committee charged with planning must be educated to the basic structure of the rite as well as all the options and taught the value of planning from the heart of the celebration outward, in spiral fashion.

*Field research.* The continuation and refinement of studies of the type that have taken place in preparation for this conference are absolutely necessary. There has to be careful follow up; there have to be questions of meaning. We have to look for the *lex agendi* as a community is studied, not just on one particular Sunday but week after week. The questions, as Peter Henriot so eloquently stated for us, are these: Is this community that meets regularly for Eucharist appreciably more just, more loving, more open to the disenfranchised, welcoming, more willing to commit themselves day after day to the work of conversion, the work of transcending love? (see p. 119f.). These are the questions that will determine the quality of liturgical reform.

*Active participation* is another area of concern for me. I found it disconcerting to read among the respondents' comments: ''I don't participate; I just listen.'' In my judgment, based on the work I've done on the liturgical movement in the United States, ''active participation'' in the minds of the liturgical reformers was the key to renewal—and it had almost nothing to do with what we do at the liturgy. It had less to do with *doing* it than *meaning* it. It had everything to do, therefore, with what was behind the expression of the Amens with which the celebration was punctuated.

Of course, it is important to care for feast and season and to have participation aids, to sing well, and to give a warm greeting of peace. But that is not the point of participation. The point of active participation is meaning it when we say, "Amen."

Allow me an aside. The liturgical movement was one phase of a larger movement in the early years of the twentieth century, a movement grounded in Scripture and theology, celebrated in liturgy, and expressed in social action. An ecclesiology of the Church as mystical body was replacing the Church as the perfect society of the nineteenth century. That kind of theology had profound ramifications for the liturgy: If we are the body of Christ, we are all co-offerers, standing around the table and celebrating with Christ, *the* leader of prayer. But even as we celebrate, we embrace the demands that "Amen" makes on us. The movement for social justice was not a separate movement, as it is in our day. It seems to me that people like Virgil Michel would be puzzled by a discussion of liturgy *and* social justice since the early pioneers of the liturgical movement simply could not conceive of the one without the other.

Other Issues, more briefly addressed:

*A feminist critique* must inform the celebration of the next twenty-five years. The only two suggestions of a new feminist consciousness in our 820 pages of data were one reference to inclusive language and one statement by a woman who felt she was receiving discriminatory treatment from the chairman of the ushers' committee.

Why was feminist consciousness simply not reflected in the survey? Possibly there were no direct questions that might have elicited this data. It is also possible that those women and men who already hold such concerns are no longer part of our worshiping community. People have simply opted out. Can we afford to lose the strength and the vigor of committed women in the Church?

*Sunday celebrations in the absence of a priest.* A directory on this topic has recently been prepared in Rome and is in the process of being translated.[9] For some, this seems to be a sign of hope: "Isn't it wonderful that lay men and women will now be able to lead us on Sundays?" Others rightly recognize that such Sunday celebrations in the absence of a priest opt for a nonsacramental Church rather than change the present discipline of ordination. The use of such a document over the next twenty-five years is only postponing the inevitable, namely, coming to terms with the lack of clergy in our communities and the need to identify those people with gifts that might be blessed to the service of the community. I would like respectfully to suggest massive noncompliance with adopting either the directory or the forms of celebration specified therein.

*Scale.* We were all touched by some of the questions Ronald Grimes raised, particularly about the roles of stillness, silence, and mystery in our celebrations. I believe these cannot be tackled in the abstract—we need to deal with them at the same time that we look at the scale of our communities.

One of the problems in this day in the American Church is that most priest-presiders are being trained in situations where small, intimate celebrations of the Eucharist are the norm, whether it is in local religious communities or small seminaries. Sociological studies have demonstrated that the size of a group is critical in terms of appropriate behavior and expectations. While most presiders of the future are being formed in small community settings, they are expected to serve large parochial assemblies. Behavior and expectations will not transfer. What I am suggesting is that one of our items for serious scholarship has to be the sociological analysis of group interaction and what legitimate expectations we can place on large groups, medium-size groups, and small groups. They will not be anything alike, I believe. Presiders will need to learn to adapt their behavior and expectations to *scale.*

Along with scale is the *question of community,* a word we so frequently employ. In the first part of this presentation, I talked about a new vocabulary that we have adopted almost effortlessly: catechesis, scrutinies, proclamation, and so on. Add to that list the word "community," a word laden with meanings and expectations. Perhaps we need to give the word "community" a rest until we sort out its various meanings and discover, on the sociological level, what different groups are capable of attaining.

*Enculturation* has only just begun. In light of Juan Sosa's presentation (see p. 121), I will not dwell on this issue except to communicate what, in my judgment, was the most shocking line in the 820 pages of the report. I refer to a community of immigrants, mostly from the Caribbean, who said they wanted a white priest in their parish, since otherwise they would feel "second-classed." I disagree with the speaker who inferred that we have embraced the idea of world Church. We are still highly European, with European models and expectations. The fact that any community wanted a white priest rather than one of its own, else it be second classed, says that we have to look not just at trilingual or bilingual celebrations or an eclectic use of different ethnic music but at the much deeper question of ethnic identity and pride and how that might be fostered in our celebrations.

Finally, the *question of catechesis and mystagogia*. By 1974 our new liturgical library of revised rites was virtually complete. In a period of about five years we had had an instructional barrage of liturgical documents, one after another. We quickly tired of the work of catechesis. It's time for new efforts in the liturgical education of our communities. Now, however, I think we need less catechesis and more profound mystagogia. That means a new commitment to *doing* the rites well—the best form of teaching. The difference between catechesis and mystagogia is that catechesis is prose and mystagogia is poetry. Mystagogia deals less with teaching but rather unfolds the symbols of our celebration in a more poetic mode, gradually forming the deeper affections of our heart.

## Conclusion

In conclusion, a word from one of the respondents who said, "I just think we have to do the best that it is possible for us to do. The only way we can do that is to try things, to be critical of them, and to encourage one another as we go along." A formula for our future work is offered here: the liturgical life of the community, together with whatever experimentation that entails, must be the subject of critical analysis in an atmosphere of mutual encouragement.

The respondent who formulated that statement knew the value of building a future agenda on the bedrock of hope. That's what I've tried to do this morning, bearing in mind the wisdom learned at a French-speaking table: People will leave our dinner parties if we are incapable of speaking in the future tense.

## Notes

1. The quotations from participants of the study *Liturgical Renewal, 1963–1988* are verbatim citations unless otherwise indicated.

2. See Austin Fleming, *Preparing for Liturgy: A Theology and Spirituality* (Washington: The Pastoral Press, 1985).

3. According to its first report, *The Notre Dame Study of Catholic Parish Life* is an interdisciplinary endeavor to understand better the American parish of the 1980s as a dynamic community. Many elements of parish life are addressed: organization, staffing, leadership, priorities, and their interrelations; liturgies and sacramental preparation; programs and participation; beliefs, values, expectations, and practices; historical, ethnographic, sociological, and religiocultural contexts. See David C. Leege and Joseph Gremillion, "The U.S. Parish Twenty Years After Vatican II: An Introduction to the Study," Report no. 1 (December 1984). The liturgical section of this study instrument became, with some alteration, the instrument used in assembling data for this Georgetown colloquium.

4. "Our Cluttered Vestibule: The Unreformed Entrance Rite," *Worship* 48 (1974), 270–277.

5. See *Egeria's Travels*, trans. and ed. John Wilkinson (London: S.P.C.K., 1971).

6. *Teaching a Stone to Talk: Expeditions and Encounters* (New York: Harper & Row, 1982) 18.

7. The National Conference of Catholic Bishops, meeting in November 1988, adopted the latter position in the publication *Guidelines for Lay Preaching*.

8. "In planning the celebration, then, the priest should consider the general spiritual good of the assembly rather than his personal outlook. He should be mindful that the choice of texts is to be made in consultation with the ministers and others who have a function in the celebration, including the faithful in regard to the parts that more directly belong to them" (GIRM, no. 313).

9. In their November 1989 plenary assembly, the National Conference of Catholic Bishops approved for liturgical use in the dioceses of the United States an *Order for Sunday Celebrations in the Absence of a Priest* (Ed.).

# *Contributors*

JOHN F. BALDOVIN, S.J., is associate professor of theology, Jesuit School of Theology at Berkeley and the Graduate Theological Union, Berkeley, California.

RONALD L. GRIMES is professor, Department of Religion and Culture, Wilfrid Laurier University, Waterloo, Ontario, Canada.

ROGER HAIGHT, S.J., is professor of theology, Regis College, Toronto, Ontario, Canada.

MONIKA K. HELLWIG is professor of theology, Georgetown University, Washington, D.C.

PETER J. HENRIOT, S.J., is the former director, The Center of Concern, Washington, D.C.

KATHLEEN HUGHES, R.S.C.J., is associate professor of liturgy, Catholic Theological Union, Chicago, Illinois.

AIDAN KAVANAGH, O.S.B., is professor of liturgics, The Divinity School, Yale University, New Haven, Connecticut.

DON E. SALIERS is former professor of liturgy, Candler School of Theology, Emory University, Atlanta, Georgia.

GERARD S. SLOYAN is professor, Department of Religion, Temple University, Philadelphia, Pennsylvania and is currently at St. John's University, Collegeville, Minnesota.

JUAN J. SOSA is director, Instituto de Liturgia Hispana, Miami, Florida.